COLOR AND DESIGN IN
MACRAMÉ

VIRGINIA I. HARVEY

VNR VAN NOSTRAND REINHOLD COMPANY

NEW YORK CINCINNATI TORONTO LONDON MELBOURNE

ACKNOWLEDGMENTS

Writing is a lonely occupation. An author must have long periods of peace and quiet to put the thoughts on paper. Inevitably, friends and family must cooperate, adjust, and take over the responsibilities of the author during this period. It is not possible to list and thank each individual, but I am most grateful for the many contributions of my family and my friends. The reader who asked my husband, Bill, to autograph a copy of the first book because she was sure "his patience was as important as her writing" was perceptive.

Book design and editing are as significant as the author's contribution in a how-to-do-it book, so I am very grateful to Nancy Newman for her patience and encouragement, and Estelle Silbermann for her skillful editing. Myron Hall, designer of the book, has taken my words and illustrations and organized them into a handsome volume that can be easily followed and clearly understood.

To all the knotters who submitted slides, shipped articles to be photographed, or had their work photographed, it is because you were willing to share that this book is a showcase for some of the best macramé being produced today. I thank you for the opportunity to bring it to my readers.

There are many colleagues at the University of Washington whom I wish to thank. From the School of Home Economics, both Dr. Mary Louise Johnson, Director, and Professor Doris Brockway, under whose direction I act as Preparator of the Costume and Textile Study Collections, have been generous with their help and understanding. Ann Johansen, my assistant, has accepted extra assignments cheerfully. From the School of Art, Spencer Moseley, Director, and Richard Proctor, Assistant Professor and Chairman of the Textile Design Division, were consulted frequently on color, design, and teaching macramé. From Audio-Visual Services, I thank Bill Eng, whose photography contributes so much to my publications and who has taken all the black and white photographs in this volume except where otherwise noted; Uwe K. Arendt, who prepared the drawings in their final form; and Malcolm Varon, who has taken all the color photographs except as otherwise noted. Also, I am grateful to the many other photographers whose work is included.

Finally, I should like to dedicate this book to my father, who taught me to be curious and then counseled me to pursue a subject in depth.

Also by the Author

Macrame: The Art of Creative Knotting
(Van Nostrand Reinhold Company, 1967)

Van Nostrand Reinhold Company Regional Offices:
New York Cincinnati Chicago Millbrae Dallas

Van Nostrand Reinhold Company International Offices:
London Toronto Melbourne

Library of Congress Catalog Card Number: 70-163313

Designed by Myron S. Hall III

Printed and bound in Japan by Zokeisha Publications, Ltd.

Published by Van Nostrand Reinhold Company
450 West 33rd Street, New York, N.Y. 10001

Published simultaneously in Canada by
Van Nostrand Reinhold Ltd.

16 15 14 13 12 11 10 9 8 7 6 5 4 3 2

CONTENTS

INTRODUCTION

Just three years ago I wrote in *Macramé: The Art of Creative Knotting,* "After many months of macramé-hunting and following many clues, I have decided that macramé could almost be classed as a dying technique. A few people are knotting and some recognize it as something they saw as children, but the majority of the people I met had neither seen it nor heard of it. It is a craft that should not be lost, so if this book serves to keep it alive, the effort of writing it will have been worth-while."

Now, no lament need be said over a macramé bier. Not only has it claimed its rightful place among the textile structures, but its use and popularity have surpassed the most extravagant predictions. Craftsmen are working with form, texture, and color to produce sculptural forms, decorative screens, wall hangings, and more functional items such as belts, handbags, tote bags, fashion trimmings, articles of clothing, and soft jewelry. Decorative articles for interiors such as room dividers, rugs, lamps, upholstery, and luggage racks are being made, and the technique has been applied to such diverse items as babies' rattles and horses' trappings.

Just as diverse are the people who are enjoying macramé. Artists who are producing spectacular sculptural forms contrast with schoolchildren who are earning spending money by knotting soft jewelry and belts for schoolmates. Fashion items made in a small factory employing college students are available in the exclusive shops, and kits for making your own belts, necklaces, and bags are available from some mail order catalogues and from stores.

This book has not been written to teach the macramé knots, but to challenge the knotter who already has a knowledge of the technique. Readers can refer to my first book, *Macramé: The Art of Creative Knotting,* to learn the basic knots, and, as a matter of fact, many of the pieces used as illustrations for this book were made by knotters who had no other source for learning the technique.

The diagrams are more schematic than realistic, because they are used to explain the relationship of the knots to each other rather than how they are tied. Chapter Two, "The Knots and How They Combine," provides a brief explanation of how the knots are tied, and will be a key to the diagrams in case of any problems interpreting them.

Every effort has been made to keep the directions as simple and clear as possible, but the principles that are discussed frequently combine several steps of knotting, and so it has been necessary to condense some of the explanations. After some experience has been gained in the technique, most knotters need less specific directions, and presumably the reader who knows the knots would prefer concise directions so that more information can be included. In fact, many knotters can reproduce a design from a photograph without any written explanation. Hopefully, by including diagrams which are frequently accompanied by photographs of the knotted piece the less experienced knotter will be able to gain this skill.

The greatest need now is for more information on color and design in macramé, and the stimulation for knotters to produce original forms and designs. This book is designed to fill those needs. Illustrations were carefully chosen to include the broadest and best selection of function, style, design, and color that could be found, and although much more might have been said if there had been more space, the material included should serve the purpose — to show the dramatic growth in macramé design and function, to stimulate more ideas and growth, and to give the knotter greater freedom and an impetus to design his own macramé.

Several approaches to color and design will be discussed, with accompanying diagrams and illustrations. Since many of the photographs illustrate several points that are discussed in different places in the text, it has not been possible to keep all related information together. Whereas in some instances, the text will refer to examples in other parts of the book, in other instances it has been left to the reader's curiosity to find them for himself.

After reading a section, the reader will find it illuminating to review all the photographs in the book to see how the many artists have used various elements in their designs. For instance, after reading about density, he should inspect each photograph and note the importance of this element in the designs, how it has been used, and how the knots have been combined to achieve the different densities.

Now that the revival of macramé has brought so much pleasure to so many, perhaps this book can open up new horizons to the knotter, so that he may bring a greater depth and variation to color and design in macramé.

1-1

1-2

1. DESIGN

Design and color in any art medium can be approached in many ways, and each approach has its own merits. For instance, design in macramé could be analyzed from the following perspectives:

1. Reduce the work to its basic element, the knot, then consider how the knots combine to form pattern.
2. Isolate the forms and motifs that are predominant in knotted pattern, then study how these motifs can be combined. Explore the variety of these combinations.
3. Inspect the surfaces, patterns, and forms in macramé to see how texture, scale, density, color, and shape are used.
4. Examine the elements of design as they appear in macramé. How are rhythm, repetition, balance, variety, and unity achieved?
5. Consider the variety of techniques that move the knotted surface from a flat, two-dimensional surface into the third dimension and sculptural form.

Although color is only one of the elements listed under the third category, it is a very important part of macramé, and must be given separate consideration. It can be understood more fully if it too is reduced to the basic element, the knot, to see how color emerges when cords of more than one color are combined. A study of some of the motifs predominant in macramé design will reveal how the color moves through the design, and when these movements are familiar, the motifs can be combined in pattern so the color is balanced and the design successful.

What sparks the urge to create a piece of macramé? Sometimes it is the material — the discovery of a new cord — or perhaps some handsome beads tease the knotter's imagination. It might be a design element — a combination of knots that form an uneven edge, or maybe a button form that challenges a craftsman to use it in a design. Perhaps a doodle scribbled on the telephone pad may form the nucleus of an idea. Frequently, it is the need for a specific article, and so the impetus may come from the need for a sturdy book bag, a room divider, or perhaps a necklace.

1-1. Braiding is combined with macramé into a sculptural wall hanging or a free-hanging piece. Robert Mills has used a smooth, twisted, plastic cord. (Photograph by Robert Lopez.)

1-2. In "Yellow Sisal with Three Tassels," a wall hanging by Gerald P. Hodge, the hairy quality of the Yucatan sisal binder twine softens the rigid geometric quality of the design. Dimensions: 16″ x 56″. (Photograph by Michael V. Przekop.)

Since an understanding of the design processes and the various factors that influence decisions will help the novice, an examination of these processes from their various starting points is worthwhile. Suppose a new knotting material has come to hand: What are the qualities of the new material? Every material has characteristics of its own that make it appealing, and a skillful designer will combine the material and the pattern into a design that will fulfill its functional requirements while retaining these characteristics and, hopefully, enhancing them.

Is the new cord shiny or dull, smooth like a firmly twisted linen or hairy like sisal? And what about size? Even a three-inch rope brings forth visions of a mammoth, sculptural knotting, while fine, delicate cords and infinite patience combine to make beautiful jewelry or cobwebby hangings and transparencies.

Then, there are the very practical considerations. Would this material wear well in a book bag? If it is used for place mats, would it wash? A design must perform the function for which it was intended, or it is not worth the time and effort to develop it.

Taking the cord in hand, the knotter should let his imagination range freely and consider tactile quality and visual characteristics. He should see how many things he can think of that this material might be used for, and not be too practical at this point, but rather see how far afield his imagination will carry him. For this is the way fresh, new ideas are born. The final design may bear no resemblance to the original idea; it may be a totally new thought because the designer was not hampered by being practical.

When an appealing idea occurs, it is wise to cut a few lengths of the new cord and knot some samples to test the pattern visualized. A note should be made of the length of these cords in each sample, so that later the amount of cords needed for a piece and their lengths can be calculated.

Designing is partly a series of selections, and to select means to accept or reject from a group — in this case to accept or reject a sample that is an attempt to combine materials and patterns into a cohesive design. Some of the samples will be rejected, and it will seem that work in them was for naught, but this is not necessarily true. Knowledge of the combinations that don't work is as important to the palette of the designer as knowledge of those that do. Sometimes designs may come from divine inspiration, but unfortunately they are usually the result of much experimenting and thought. It was a temptation to add "hard work," but solving a problem is not really hard work when it means creating something that is totally a product of the imagination. Its completion is a challenge, and each discovery of a part that contributes to the whole is an exciting event. And when the end result is a design that is pleasing to the eye, it brings a very special sense of satisfaction. Of course, not every design will be completely successful, but an occasional one suffices to nurture the creative urge.

Getting back to the samples, it is important to look at them critically in order to decide whether those beautiful qualities that made the yarn appealing are still there. If it is a smooth yarn, perhaps the emphasis is on the pattern, so the material is chosen to make it crisp and clear-cut. On the other hand, a more textured cord may soften the design, and perhaps that is the effect the designer will want. When the combination that satisfies all requirements has been found, the sample will provide the key to the piece as a whole. More planning may be necessary to complete the design, but an idea is born.

Perhaps, in an exhibition, a piece that combined the knots in a new and different way stirred a knotter's imagination. For example, the solidly knotted triangle shown in Fig. 1-3 will combine with other such triangles to make an irregular edge. If several pieces with irregular edges were knotted and then hung side by side, the designer could employ the use of positive-negative space or "notan" in his design. This was the impulse that sparked the design in Fig. 1-4, where the pattern in the spaces between the knotted pieces is as important to the design as the knotted areas themselves. In this work, changes in density and other knot combinations are some of the other elements that give variety to the uneven edges. Color was also an important consideration, and variety, repetition, unity, rhythm, and other elements of design were all kept in mind as the work progressed.

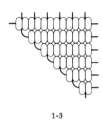

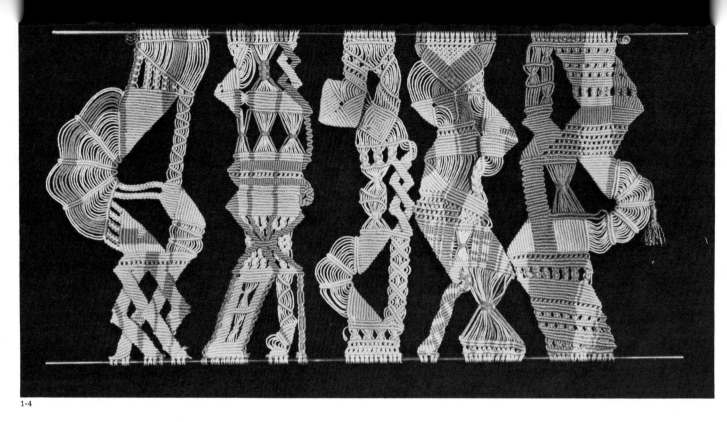

1-4. Deep gold and white silk was knotted by the author in five separate pieces and then arranged on two brass rods, which can be rearranged any time, and thus the viewer can participate in the design. Dimensions: 12″ x 24″.

1-4

No doubt, most frequently a design stems from a need, and although "form follows function" is one of the oldest cliches of the designer's vocabulary, it is nonetheless true. It may also be the easiest approach to designing. If, for instance, a room divider is needed, the limitations of the problem are immediately apparent. It must screen without closing completely, and in an area of heavy traffic, it might be bumped, so it must be relatively sturdy. In addition, to be practical, it must be cleanable and preferably not too much of a dust-catcher. So far, we have a sturdy material that will clean. Next, to break an interior space without completely blocking the vision, a pattern with some open spaces would be desirable. Does this mean solidly knotted areas contrasted with spaces that are entirely open, or will those spaces be filled with unknotted cords? Since the cord is to be silhouetted, then

perhaps it should have some surface interest such as a thick and thin texture, or maybe the scale of a heavy rope would be more interesting. Decisions on pattern and material are interdependent, and some experimenting may be necessary before the best choice is made.
The inexperienced, impatient designer, will too frequently settle for less than the best choice because he doesn't want to take the time or make the effort to explore all the possibilities. Inevitably, the results are disappointing in these cases, and not worth all the time spent on the project. Although burning with enthusiasm, the designer should not skimp on planning time. Of course, as his experience grows, the time needed for planning will be reduced, since he will then have a more thorough knowledge of materials and techniques.
Once the idea is there, how does it become a design? Going back to the

1-5

1-6

1-5. Almost-white linen has been combined with wood beads in an elegant and practical tote bag by Ruth Payn. Dimensions: Approximately 12″ x 10″ x 2″.

1-6. Carol Robinson has achieved complete unity between the pottery bell and the strap from which it hangs. (Photograph by Lincoln Potter.)

1-7. In the "Alhambra Pattern," the author combined white linen cords and wood beads in an open pattern. Complete directions for this pattern are given in the December 1969 issue of *Threads in Action*.

1-7

room divider first, if a simple, repetitive pattern such as the one in Fig. 1-7 is chosen, then the material is selected, the frame prepared, and the knotting cords calculated and cut. The record of the length of the cords in the sample will give the ratio of take-up for the knotting and the number of ends necessary for the width of the piece. If the designer chooses to attach the cords directly to the frame and work within it, then there is no doubt that the knotting will fit the frame; however, sometimes it is difficult to place the frame in a position comfortable for knotting. The alternative is to knot the piece on a rigid knotting base that is porous enough to hold pins; for example, some of the fiber wallboards are excellent knotting bases. Sufficient cords for the width of the piece, cut long enough to complete it, are mounted on the fiberboard. This base must be slightly wider than the frame, but it

1-8

1-9

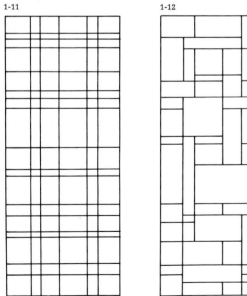

1-11

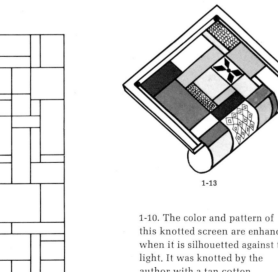

1-12

1-13

1-10. The color and pattern of this knotted screen are enhanced when it is silhouetted against the light. It was knotted by the author with a tan cotton upholsterer's cord and faceted glass beads in topaz and smoke color. Dimensions: 18″ x 40″.

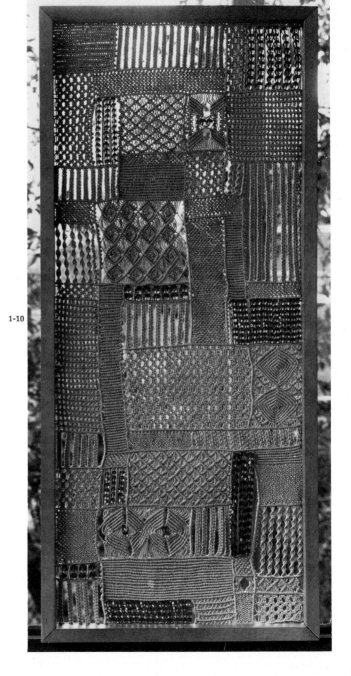

1-10

should only be 24″ to 30″ high so that it can be handled easily in a sitting position if it is braced against a table or some other support. (See Fig. 1-8.) When all the space on the board is filled with knotting, then the completed part is moved up and the work repinned to continue. This process is repeated until the desired length is reached.

Some method of suspending the work, such as hanging it from a doorway as shown in Fig. 1-9 is another alternative, but it is difficult to keep an exact dimension unless the knotting is pinned to a surface. If the knotter prefers to work this way, perhaps the wall hanging could be installed without a frame. All the various alternatives should be considered in planning the piece.

If an over-all plan for the screen is not satisfying, then the space within the screen as a whole must also be considered for the design. The variety of possible designs are as numerous as the designers, but a few general suggestions might be helpful.

Macramé lends itself very well to horizontal, vertical, and diagonal space divisions, but free forms and curvilinear lines may be created easily too. Density and texture are important elements in macramé design, and the screen in Fig. 1-10 was composed with these particular elements in mind.

The design was planned on a large piece of butcher paper on which the dimensions of the frame were drawn. Keeping in mind the principles of variety, repetition, balance, and rhythm, the space was divided horizontally and vertically, as shown in Fig. 1-11. Then parts of the lines were erased, both vertically and horizontally (see Fig. 1-12) to change the shapes of the rectangles formed, still remembering to keep them balanced but not too static. When a pleasing space division was achieved, attention was then turned to the density of the separate rectangles. Construction paper in black, shades of gray, and white were cut and superimposed over the rectangles. When the arrangement was balanced, the completed design was ready to be translated into the knotted screen.

After the top section of the cartoon had been pinned to the board, with the remainder of the design rolled and pinned to the back of the board (as shown in Fig. 1-13) the knotting was begun. A black section indicated a solidly knotted area, dark grays were moderately dense, and the density decreased as the paper became lighter. White areas had no knots at all. The few motifs that were used in some rectangles were indicated on the original cartoon, then knotted into the design as the knotting progressed over the rectangle on which they were drawn. The procedure followed in designing the room divider has been

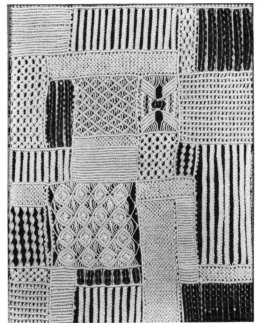

1-14

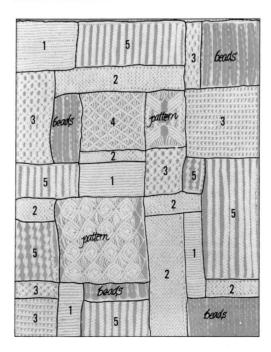

1-14. The density of the knotting is indicated by numbers: 1 is the greatest density, and it then decreases down to the most open areas, which are 5. The full screen is shown in Fig. 1-10.

1-16

1-15. This charming couple is the center of a pin cushion that was made at the Refredi School of Embroidery in Florence, Italy. The knotted section measures 2¾″ x 1⅞″, and it is a part of the School of Home Economics' Costume and Textile Study Collections at the University of Washington.

1-16. Areas of knotting spaced on a background of unknotted cords make a very handsome composition in this piece knotted of a viscose rug yarn by Mary Stephens Nelson.

explained at some length as an example; however, there are many other ways a design might have been made. Although these steps may not be appropriate for the next piece you plan, they do show that the designing was a logical, problem-solving sequence. Another designer might prefer a free design that could be sketched, and a different medium such as paint or ink. The general plan might be a geometric space division, a single motif repeated in different sizes, colors, textures, or some combination of all of these elements. Many designs are geometric because the knots combine very logically in rectangles, diamonds, triangles, and other simple motifs. In single macramé motifs, curvilinear designs are frequently found and they can be used very effectively in larger-scale designs. In fact, macramé is versatile enough to use simplified pictorial motifs if the theme of the design so requires. (Fig. 1-15.)

In contrast to the strictly disciplined method of working from a preplanned design, many very successful pieces of macramé have been designed by arbitrarily choosing a given number of cords, attaching them to a holding cord, a dowel, or whatever strikes the designer's fancy, and then knotting freely, by whim. Fig. 1-4 was designed by this method, and "The Frail Grail" shown on page 71 was designed as it was knotted. For this approach to succeed, the designer must be willing to unknot when a completed section does not fit the space or relate to the rest of the piece. Many knotters who work this way say the knotting carries the designer along as though it had a mind of its own. This fascinating method — or really lack of method — leads to discoveries of knot-combinations and cord-manipulations that would never occur in a preplanned work.

When working this way, it is easier for the designer and gives him a greater sense of freedom if he approaches the work with the feeling that it is expendable. He should be knotting just for the pleasure of it, not to accomplish six inches of knots per hour, or to complete a wall hanging for a birthday gift when the birthday is tomorrow. When working against a deadline, there must be planning! If the design that has been devised without planning proves unsuccessful, and there are too many knots to remove before a change and an improvement can be made, it shouldn't be continued. The designer should discard the piece, but profit from his mistakes. He should weigh the value of the material in the piece against the value of his time and remember that the experience, particularly if he knows why the design was not successful, is very valuable. For such lessons money is paid to teachers and frequently the lesson is not learned until it is experienced anyway. Since knotting by whim is a gamble, it certainly isn't for everyone, but the rewards are great when a piece is successful. To approach a design this way, most of us must completely reorient our reasons for designing, and regard it as a form of play, just as you might spend an afternoon playing a game of golf or walking on the beach. Sometimes, nothing is left from the time and effort except the pleasant memory. If the piece is unsuccessful, was the material any more costly than the fee to play golf, or the trip to the beach? Whether or not the result is successful, one of the greatest rewards is discovering one's inventiveness.

Many knotters find that it is easier to design with macramé than with some of the other textile techniques, and in the going over of some of the elements that create a design, perhaps we can learn why this is. Books on design list rhythm, repetition, variety, balance, unity, texture, size, shape, mass, and space as some elements of design.

Certainly, the knots in themselves form a rhythm and a repetition, and an obvious example is the triangular motif that is a part of the "Alhambra Pattern," with its rhythmic progression of repeated knots. (See Fig. 1-7.) Many other examples of these principles can be found in knotted pieces.

As for variety, is there a photograph in this book in which the piece does not show variety? How can a piece be knotted without some variety?

Balance is in the designer's hands, but he is aided by many of the characteristics of macramé. The diagonal line that is created so frequently and sometimes unconsciously by the knotter brings balance to his designs, as do knot repetition and combinations.

The repetition of the knots; the way the knots combine in diagonals; the pattern of the unknotted cords repeating a lineal pattern — these are just a few of the unifying elements to be found in an analysis of a knotted pattern.

Although the delicate balance within a macramé pattern can very easily be destroyed by introducing another material, for some reason the temptation seems to be greater in macramé than in other techniques to combine shells, driftwood, leaves, moss, beads, bells — yes, even pretzels — in the knotting. With skillful designing, it is possible to combine materials very successfully; however, for every good design there must be at least ten that do not unify. Macramé with beads, bones, rocks, or pretzels can be handsome, but the designer should proceed carefully and thoughtfully. If the material combined looks "stuck in" or if it is too dominant, then the unity is destroyed. Any added ingredient should look like it belongs, like it is at home in its environment. This may not be easy, but it is definitely a challenge!

1-17. Tensolite, a fine plastic yarn, has been used by Judith M. Hendry to create a handsome pair of earrings that feature contrast of the dense areas against open Square Knotted pattern. (Photograph by Paul Macapia.)

1-18. "Locust II" (detail). Francoise Grossen has used a dramatic contrast in the scale of the knotting materials in this monumental hanging. (Photograph by Stan Ries.)

One of macramé's strongest and most appealing qualities is texture. There is some danger that highly textured yarns will compete with a strongly textured knotted pattern, but usually the knotter will reject a yarn that hides a beautiful pattern, or keep the pattern simple to show off a handsome yarn.

Scale, or size, is also the choice of the designer. Usually this depends upon the size of the materials used. In fact, scale of the knotted piece and the yarns that are used to make it are interrelated and both must be considered in the designing. The eyesight and patience of the designer will determine the size of the finer yarns that are knotted. Delicate, ethereal pieces like Judith Hendry's earrings (Fig. 1-17) or sturdy, sculptural pieces like the author's "Frail Grail" can be fashioned from yarns almost as fine as human hair. Knotting with these is not difficult, but good eyesight and a steady hand is needed to remove errors. Heavy ropes looped around each other, sometimes so simply they hardly qualify as macramé, are lovely sculptures (Fig. 1-18).

Contrast in the scale of the materials used is another effective device in designing. Usually, yarns of equal size are used in a piece, but the combination of different sizes achieves a very different texture and an interesting silhouette when used in a transparency. (See Fig. 1-19.)

Scale pertains to the size of the piece that is being designed as well as the materials that are used in it. Not only is Francoise Grossen's monumental hanging shown on page 62 beautiful in itself, but the drama of its scale also commands attention.

Interesting shapes can be created in many ways in knotting, since more freedom is possible within this technique for shaping than, for instance, in weaving. Woven fabric, except in cases of some special manipulation, is limited to the horizontal and vertical of the loom, but two-dimensional macramé need not conform to the rectangular shape, and three-dimensional knotting can take almost any form the imagination dictates. When placed side by side, mass and space frequently refer to the relationship of positive and negative space, or the quality of notan. The solidity of some of the knotted areas contrasted with the open spaces created when cords are withdrawn from one space to knot the solid form in another adds notan to many knotted designs, and the freedom in shaping that is possible in macramé gives the designer the option to work with notan. It was this quality that played an important part in the design of the piece in Fig. 1-4.

With all these elements of design so available within the technique itself, even an inexperienced craftsman with some sensitivity can create successful designs in macramé.

1-19. The variety of scale and texture of the knotting materials in this hanging (knotted by Erika Binz in a textile course taught by Marlise Staehelin at AGS Basel, Switzerland) has created a handsome and unusual piece, particularly when viewed with light behind it as in this photograph. (Photograph by Hans Isenschmid.)

2. RECOGNIZING THE MACRAMÉ KNOTS

Macramé is deceptive. To the novice, it looks like a very complex combination of knots that would take a long time to learn and extensive practice to master, when nothing could be further from the truth. Its popularity proves this, for if macramé were as difficult as it looks, only the very persistent would be knotting. Many handsome designs that appear to be very complicated are knotted with the Double Half Hitch only, while others may be exclusively Square Knots. One of the two loops that are used to make the Double Half Hitch can be repeated, giving a different effect, such as a chain or a Reversed Half Hitch. The Overhand Knot and the Josephine Knot appear occasionally, and each can be used alone to make a knotted structure, or either one may be combined with other knots.

The knots can be learned with a few hours' practice, and after they are mastered, it is a matter of learning the many ways they combine in pattern and shaping. With experience, it is possible to reproduce a macramé pattern from a photograph, providing the knots are shown clearly, and Chapter 3 has been included to make it possible to recognize the knots in a photograph, and to show the forms they produce when combined. First, however, for the beginner and also for the more advanced knotter who may need it, here is a review of the knots themselves.

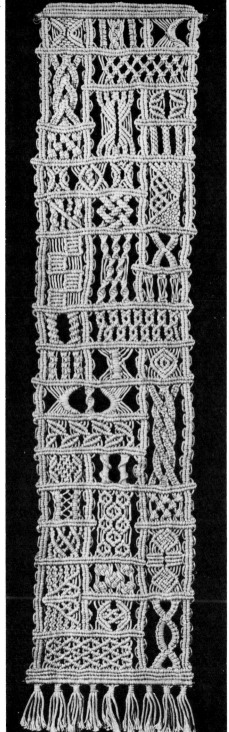

2-1. Joan Michaels Paque employed natural-colored polished cotton in "Montage."

The Half Knot

Place the right-hand cord 4 over the core cords 2 and 3 and leave it in that position. Pick up the left-hand cord 1, place it over cord 4, then bend it around 4, continue under 2 and 3 diagonally, and bring it out through the space between cords 3 and 4. Pull the knotting cords firmly and repeat to form a sinnet of Half Knots that spirals.

2-5

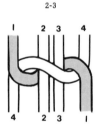

2-3

2-4

2-6

2-2. Half Knot sinnet.

2-3. The Half Knot.

2-4. Two Half Knots.

2-5. Half Knot sinnets tied until they turn once; then the cords are regrouped and they are tied again until they turn once.

2-6. Half Knot sinnets tied until they turn once and in alternate directions. The rows of sinnets are separated with a row of Square Knots.

2-7. Half Knot sinnets tied until they turn once and arranged in a diamond shape in a background of Square Knots.

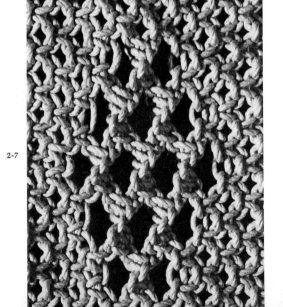

2-7

2-8. A very simple, small hanging knotted on a rectangular wire frame by Judith M. Hendry. Dimensions: Approximately 2″ x 7½″. (Photograph by Paul Macapia.)

2-9. The simplicity of the Half Knot pattern adds dignity and
elegance to this handsome bag that was knotted by J. I. Cochran
in tan polished cotton. Dimensions: 9½" x 4" x 6".

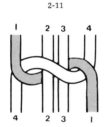

The Square Knot

The Square Knot is made in two operations. The first part is the Half Knot. For the second part, place the right-hand cord under cords 2 and 3 horizontally and leave it in that position. Pick up the left-hand cord 4, place it under the right-hand cord 1, then bend it around 1 and lay it over cords 2 and 3 diagonally and continue by pulling it down through the space between 3 and 1. Pull the knotting cords firmly and repeat the two steps alternately to form a Square Knot sinnet.

2-11   2-12

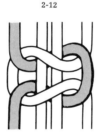

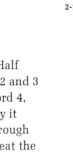

2-10. Square Knot sinnet.

2-11. The Half Knot.

2-12. The Square Knot.

2-13. In each of the rows of knots a Square Knot laid to the right is alternated with a Square Knot laid to the left.

2-14. In this bag, knotted by J. I. Cochran in white seine twine, the background for the diamond patterns in the lower portion is knotted with Square Knots that have been laid alternately to the right and then to the left. Dimensions without the handles: 13″ x 10″ x 5″.

2-15. Each row of knots moves over one cord instead of the customary two cords that create a Square Knot pattern with the knots in alternate arrangement. By moving over one cord, a twill pattern of knots is created.

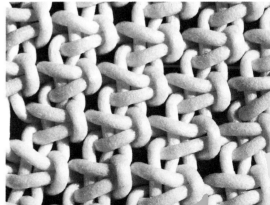

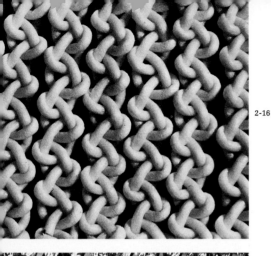

2-16

2-17

2-18

The Half Hitch

The single loop of the Half Hitch is used in several ways. It is tied with the right hand by looping it over a single cord or a group of cords, going from right to left over the cords, then around behind them from left to right and forward over itself. With the left hand, it is reversed, going over the core from left to right, behind it from right to left and forward over itself.

2-19

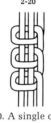
2-20

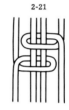
2-21

2-19. A single loop over a cord.

2-20. A single cord looped repeatedly over a cord will form a spiral.

2-21. Two cords over a core to knot a braid.

Chain

2-22

2-23

2-24

2-22. The right cord looped over the left.

2-23. Left over right.

2-24. Double cords form a double chain.

2-25

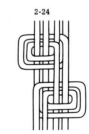

2-16. Single chains side by side, knotted of rayon olefin welting cord.

2-17. Double chains side by side knotted of rayon Macrochain.

2-18. Spirals knotted side by side of rayon Machrochain.

2-25. A braid knotted with a single loop alternately from each side over a core of two cords.

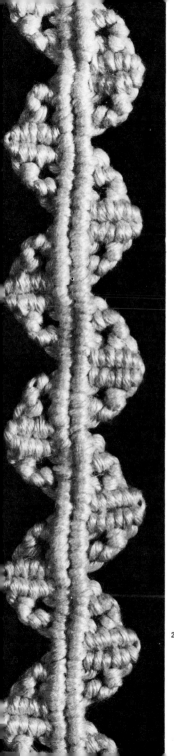

The Double Half Hitch

2-27

2-27. The Horizontal Double Half Hitch.

2-28

2-28. From right to left, knot with the right hand.

2-29

2-29. From left to right, knot with the left hand.

2-30

2-30. Two rows of Horizontal Double Half Hitches.

2-31

2-31. The Vertical Double Half Hitch.

2-32

2-32. From right to left, knot with the left hand.

2-33

2-33. From left to right, knot with the right hand.

2-34

2-34. Two rows of Vertical Double Half Hitches.

2-35

2-35. The Diagonal Double Half Hitch.

2-36

2-36. From right to left, knot with the right hand.

2-37

2-37. From left to right, knot with the left hand.

2-38

2-38. Beginning a row of Diagonal Double Half Hitches.

Cord 2 is the knotting cord. Cord 1 is the knot bearer or holding cord, and it is always crossed over the top of the knotting cord. Also, cord 1 is always held taut so the loops formed by cord 2 circle around it.

Knotting the Horizontal Double Half Hitch from right to left, the knot bearer is held in the left hand. The knotting cord is looped in a clockwise direction over 1, behind it, then in front of the loop. The same loop is repeated a second time. Reverse the directions to knot from left to right.

The Double Half Hitch is always tied exactly this same way, with these two loops, regardless of the direction. The secret of varying the direction without confusion is to be sure each two cords, as you start the knot, are in the correct position. The knot-bearing cord must be on top, so: In the Horizontal Knot, the horizontal cord is on top. In the Vertical Knot, the vertical cord is on top. In the Diagonal Knot, the diagonal cord is on top.

2-26. A braid knotted entirely with the Double Half Hitch. Three cords are knotted from side to side across a core of two cords.

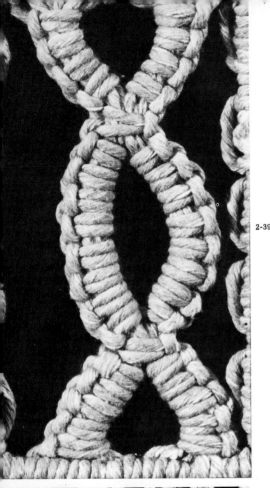

2-39

2-40

The Reversed Double Half Hitch

To knot a Reversed Double Half Hitch with a double cord, the loop is folded forward over the two strands; then another cord, usually a holding cord, is placed through the loops.

Knotting the Reversed Double Half Hitch continuously in a single cord over a cord of another cord or cords, the first knot is a Half Hitch. The knotting cord goes over the core, under it, and forward over itself. The next loop is reversed — under the core, over it, then back into the space between the two cords and down under the cord leading from the first Half Hitch.

2-41

2-41. A folded cord looped over a knot-bearing cord.

2-42

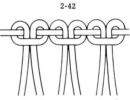

2-42. Used as a mounting knot.

2-43

2-44

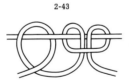

2-43, 2-44. Knotted continuously with a single cord over a knot-bearing cord.

2-39. Joan Michaels Paque has used the Reversed Double Half Hitch to form the ovals and the Square Knot where they join.

2-40. A pattern of Reversed Double Half Hitches that forms a lattice between the rows of knots.

2-45. A braid of Reversed Double Half Hitches in red and white rayon Macrochain.

2-45

22

The Overhand Knot

The Overhand Knot is tied by forming a loop, wrapping the cord around itself, and pulling the end through the loop. Two cords can move around themselves to form an Overhand Knot in a double cord, or two cords can be tied with an Overhand Knot by tying one cord over the other.

2-46

2-46. A braid of Overhand Knots in red and white rayon Macrochain.

2-51

2-47

2-47. In a single cord.

2-48

2-48. In two cords.

2-52

2-49

2-49. One cord over another, knotted with the right hand.

2-50

2-50. One cord over another, knotted with the left hand.

2-53

2-51. Overhand Knots in alternate arrangement. Knotted with pairs of cords.

2-52. Overhand Knots in a twill progression. Knotted in groups of four cords, each row of knots moves one cord to the left.

2-53. Overhand Knots in a spaced alternate arrangement that resembles netting. Both single and double rows of knots are shown.

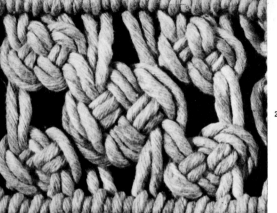

2-54

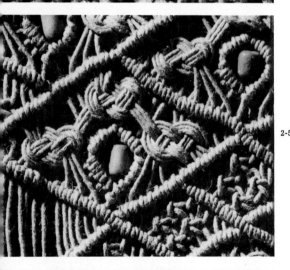

2-55

2-56

The Josephine Knot

2-63. A braid of Josephine Knots.

Two cords, or the two ends of a cord are used to tie the Josephine Knot. A loop is made with one cord, and the other cord is interwoven into it. Cord A is looped in a counterclockwise direction, with the loop to the right and the ends on the left. Cord B is placed under the loop, intersecting it at a 45° angle. The left end of cord B is woven in a clockwise direction over the lower end of A, under the upper end, then over the upper part of the loop, under itself (cord B), and finally over the lower edge of the loop. In a sinnet of Josephine Knots, alternate knots must be reversed to keep it from twisting.

2-57

2-57. Loop cord A.

2-58

2-58. Cord B is placed under the loop.

2-59

2-59. B goes over A.

2-60

2-60. Under A.

2-61

2-61. Over A.

2-62

2-62. Under itself and over A.

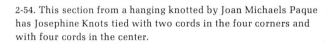

2-54. This section from a hanging knotted by Joan Michaels Paque has Josephine Knots tied with two cords in the four corners and with four cords in the center.

2-55. Josephine Knots are tied with three cords in this detail from a hanging knotted by Dolores Schiffert. (Photograph by Robert Lopez.)

2-56. These Josephine Knots of rayon Macrochain are tied in alternate arrangement.

2-63

3. COMBINING THE MACRAMÉ KNOTS

Learning the knots of macramé is the first step, and it is possible to make an infinite number of things and to achieve a wide variety of effects without progressing beyond this basic knowledge. Some of the most beautiful macramé pieces that were dependent upon texture or color for interest have been knotted of repeated Square Knots or Double Half Hitches. The simplicity of the single element is part of the beauty. However, to be limited to the rudiments is like tasting one cheese, finding it good, and deciding that one is satisfied — without ever knowing the many flavors in those left untasted.

After the discovery that basic knowledge of the knots is not enough, the next step is to learn how these knots combine to make motifs or textures, then how the motifs can be fitted together to make designs. This chapter explains only some of the ways to combine the knots, for it would take a much longer book to explore all of the possible combinations. However, familiarity with some of the basic combinations herein illustrated will make it possible to analyze many knotted structures and reproduce them when desired. The knotter will thereby have the necessary knowledge of the structure so that he can design more freely with the technique and, with further experimentation, have the joy of discovering other combinations himself.

In most cases, units using only a few cords have been chosen to illustrate the principles because the drawings are simpler and easier to understand. However, all of these units can be expanded, and usually they can be reduced. For instance, the wheel motif on page 41 could be enlarged into a round place mat by starting with many cords instead of the five cords shown in the illustrations.

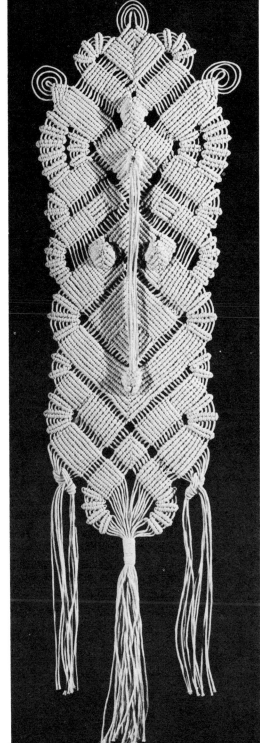

3-1. Mary Stephens Nelson composed this simple hanging almost entirely of Diagonal Double Half Hitches.

The Vertical Double Half Hitch   3-2

The Horizontal Double Half Hitch 3-3

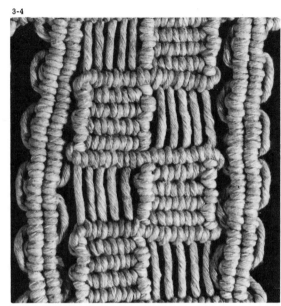

3-4

3-4. Horizontal and Vertical Double Half Hitches were used by Joan Michaels Paque for the pattern in this section of a wall hanging.

3-5. The design shown in Fig. 3-6 has been knotted of rayon satin cord.

3-5

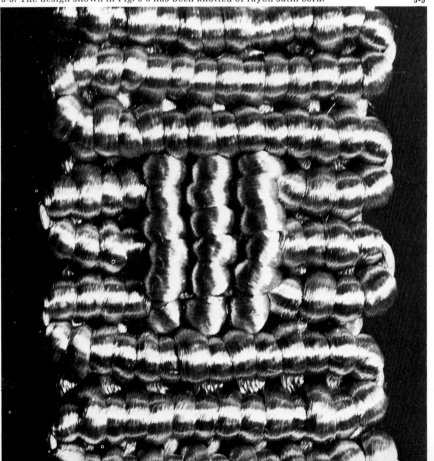

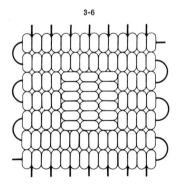

3-6

Horizontal and Vertical Double Half Hitch Combined

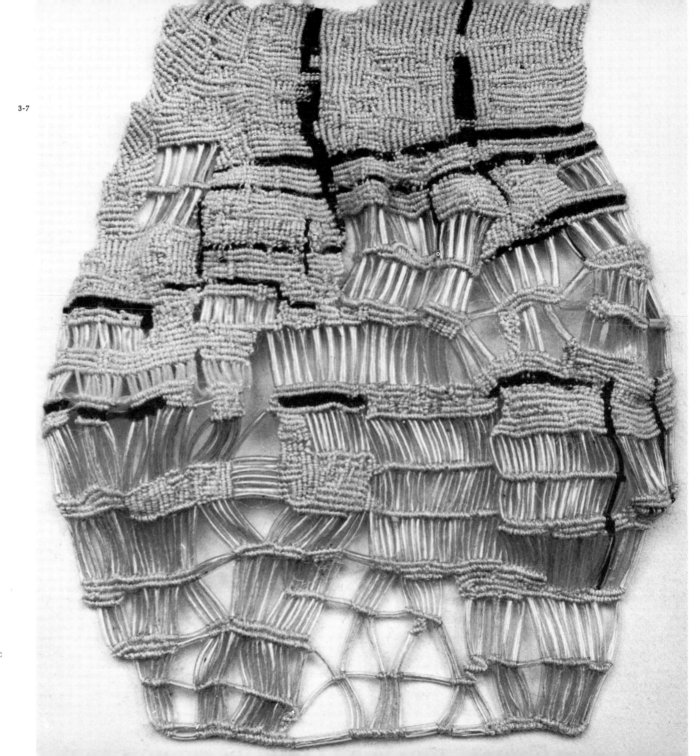

3-7. In "The World Egg" by Ed
Rossbach, Horizontal and
Vertical Double Half Hitches
have been combined with plastic
tubing in a handsome and
unusual composition.
(Photograph by Ed Rossbach.)

The Diagonal Double Half Hitch

 3-8

In a row:  3-9

With the second row reversed:   3-10

Repeated to form a texture: 3-11

3-12

In an X: 3-13

In a row of Xs  3-14

to form a braid: 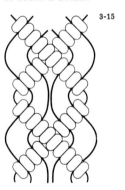 3-15

If the knots are tightened firmly, the Xs will soften and become smoothly flowing curved lines.

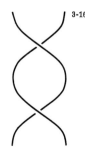 3-16

3-12. Rows of Diagonal Double Half Hitches alternated in direction as shown in Fig. 3-11.

3-17. A braid of Xs knotted with four cords.

3-18. This pottery bottle, which was knotted by Joan Michaels Paque, is embellished with braids of Xs laced together.

3-17

3-18

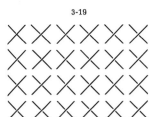

The Xs repeated form a grid:

3-20. The grid is a part of the
screen shown in Fig. 1-10.

Two rows of softened Xs repeated in alternate arrangement form a
graceful pattern of ovals.

The X is lost but the oval remains.

3-23

The Xs can be knotted so they form motifs resembling four-petaled flowers. This motif was used as the dominant pattern for the bag knotted by J. I. Cochran.

3-24. Interwoven rows of Diagonal Double Half Hitches knotted of a brown waxed linen upholsterer's twine.

3-25. A single row of Diagonal Double Half Hitches.

3-26. A simplified version of the interwoven grid.

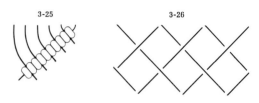

3-25   3-26

3-24

The lines of the X motif can be knotted so they interweave.

3-27. Double rows of Diagonal Double Half Hitches knotted of a brown waxed linen upholsterer's twine.

3-28. A double row of Diagonal Double Half Hitches.

3-29. A simplified version of the grid with double rows.

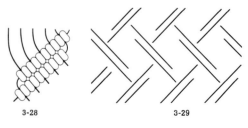

3-28   3-29

3-27

The interwoven effect is broken when a second row is knotted below the first diagonal row. When these two rows are curved to form a leaf motif, an attractive pattern results.

3-30

3-30. Double rows of Diagonal Double Half Hitches curved to form a leaf outline.

Elongate the X for a different effect:

3-31

3-32

3-32. Three diagonals will elongate it further.

3-34. The section above the bulge of this bottle, covered by Walter H. McBride, has been knotted in a pattern of elongated Xs. (Photograph by Robinson Studio.)

3-33. Elongated Xs are positioned alternately to form a pattern.

3-33

3-34

Start with a diagonal toward the left:

3-35

Add a second row and bring the holding cord from the previous row down as the last knotting cord, thus maintaining the same number of knots in each row:

3-36

If more rows are added, a parallelogram is formed.

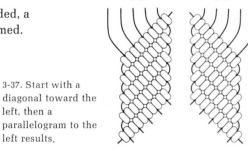
3-37   3-38

3-37. Start with a diagonal toward the left, then a parallelogram to the left results.

3-38. Start with a diagonal toward the right, then a parallelogram to the right results.

When the holding cord from each row is not used in the subsequent row, the rows are shortened progressively by one knot, and a triangle is formed.

3-40   3-41

3-40. A triangle with a left diagonal.

3-41. A triangle with a right diagonal.

3-42. Rows of triangular motifs have been repeated in an eyeglass case of rayon chainette knotted by Marjorie DeGarmo.

3-39

3-39. An arrangement of parallelograms in a knotted pattern.

When the holding cord and the last knotting cord are not used in the subsequent row, the rows are shortened progressively by two knots, and a smaller triangle results. This motif is used most often when it is necessary to change the angle of knotting from a diagonal direction to a horizontal one.

3-43   3-44

3-43. A smaller triangle with a left diagonal.

3-44. A smaller triangle with a right diagonal.

33

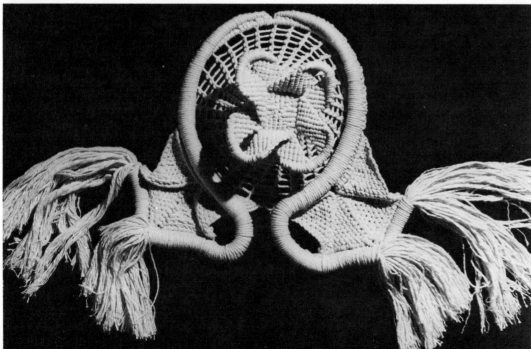

3-45, 3-46. Joan Michaels Paque has used the parallelogram to form the center of a small sculptural piece. The flowerlike motif has been placed on an open background that was made with a looping technique. Many ends have been covered with Double Half Hitches to form the circular frame and another combination of looping has been used for the wings at the sides. (Photographs 3-45 and 3-46 by Joan Michaels Paque.)

3-47. Parallelograms of three shades of green rayon satin cord form a belt.

Combine the diagonals in three similar motifs:

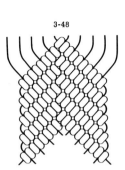

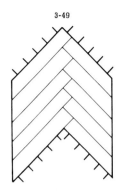

Adjacent Parallelograms

Knot a diagonal to the left, then use the first knotting cord from that row as a holding cord for a diagonal to the right. A left diagonal is next, then a right diagonal, always using the first knotting cord from the previous row as the holding cord. When each row is completed, the holding cord from the previous row is knotted on the row below it, thus maintaining the same number of knots in each row.

When it is desirable to knot adjacent parallelogram motifs in the reverse position, the diagonal of the first row on each side is reversed. The diagrams show the left diagonal knotted first with the cord at the far left acting as a holding cord. Then the diagonal on the right side is knotted and the two diagonals are joined when the holding cord from the left diagonal is used to make the last knot of the right-hand row. The first knotting cord of the left diagonal will become the holding cord for the next row, and all of the knotting cords from the previous row will be knotted on it in sequence. The last knot of the diagonal will be the holding cord from the first row on the right side of the figure; thus the rows interlock. A diagonal on the right side is next, using the first knotting cord of the previous row as the holding cord. This sequence is repeated, knotting rows on alternate sides until the figure is as large as desired.

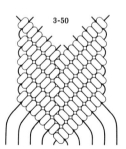

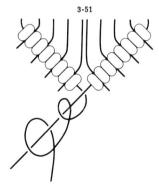

3-50. Adjacent parallelograms reversed.

3-51. Beginning a reversed parallelogram.

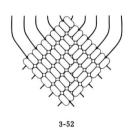 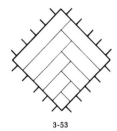

Diamonds

Knot the first two rows as in the adjacent parallelograms. The subsequent rows are knotted in the same sequence, but the figure is smaller and it becomes a diamond because each holding cord is not used again after the row is completed. Thus the rows become shorter and shorter and a diamond is formed.

3-47

Concentric Squares

The rows are knotted in the same sequence again, but for this figure, the last knotting cord is not used as well as each holding cord, so the upper part of the figure becomes a triangle. Then the lower part of the figure is formed by starting in the center and knotting each successive row toward the outer edge, again alternating from side to side like the former figures.

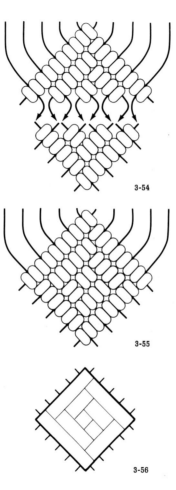

3-54

3-55

3-56

3-57. This necklace by the author combines blue tensolite and old glass beads and has the concentric square as its center motif.

3-57

A triangle is knotted by reducing each row by one knot, just as some of the triangles on the previous pages were knotted. This time a row of Horizontal Double Half Hitches is the first row, then the first knotting cord on one side becomes the holding cord for the next row. If the holding cord is taken from the left side, the hypotenuse (the longest side) of the triangle will be on the left side and all of the knotting cords will be hanging from the right side of the triangle when it is completed. If the holding cord is taken from the right, then the long side will be on the right, and the knotting cords will hang from the left. Therefore, if you want your knotting to move to the right, the holding cord will be held in the right hand. It is picked up from the left edge and held across the knotting cords. If it should move to the left, then pick up the holding cord from the right and hold it in the left hand, across the cords that are to be knotted on it.

To design freely with these knotted triangles, it is necessary to work with them until you can move the knotting in the direction you wish. Sometimes this simple rule will be helpful:

To move to the right, the holding cord must be in the right hand; to move to the left, the holding cord must be in the left hand.

Another rule that must be remembered:

When a row is completed, the holding cord is not used again until the triangle is completed and the next triangle is knotted.

It is best to place each holding cord over a pin, or in some way keep it away from the knotting area, to be sure it is not used until the triangle is finished. When only one knot remains at the point, the triangle is completed.

When the first triangle is completed, the work should be turned a quarter turn so the knotting cords are hanging toward the knotter and the second triangle is knotted at a right angle to the first one. Again, a choice must be made concerning the direction the triangle will go. If the holding cord is taken from the point of the triangle, the figure will become a larger triangle composed of the two triangles. Upon completion, the knotting cords will be hanging in the opposite direction from when the work was started.

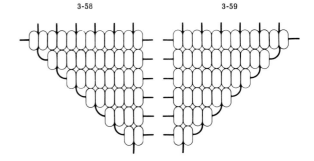

3-58   3-59

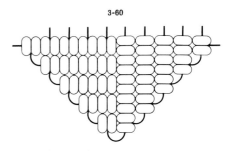

3-60

If the holding cord is taken from the right angle of the triangle, the figure will be a parallelogram, and the knotting cords will be hanging in the same direction as they were when the work was started, but they will have moved to the right (or to the left, depending upon the direction of the first triangle) a distance that is equal to the width of the triangle.

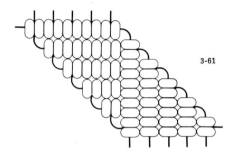

3-61

If each successive triangle is started by taking the first holding cord from the right-angle side of the previous triangle, a band of triangles will be knotted.

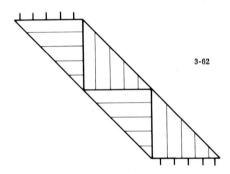

3-62

3-65. This child's toy by Judith Noble was knotted by making spirals from triangles. The toy enchants a child by expanding and contracting like an accordion. Dimensions: approximately 1¼" square by 4½" long.

When the holding cord is taken from the point of the previous triangle, and several triangles are knotted, the work turns back on itself. Four, or sometimes five triangles, will bring you back to the starting place — four if the triangles are knotted so they are true right angles, five if the angle is slightly less than a right angle, as it sometimes is. If more triangles are knotted after the work has completed a circle, a spiral will result and triangles will be knotted over the previous ones. For instance, triangle 5 will be knotted on top of, but completely free of 1. Six will be on top of 2, and so on.

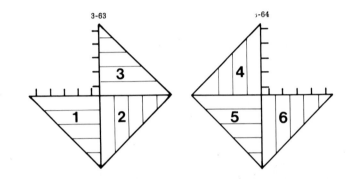

3-63

3-64

3-65

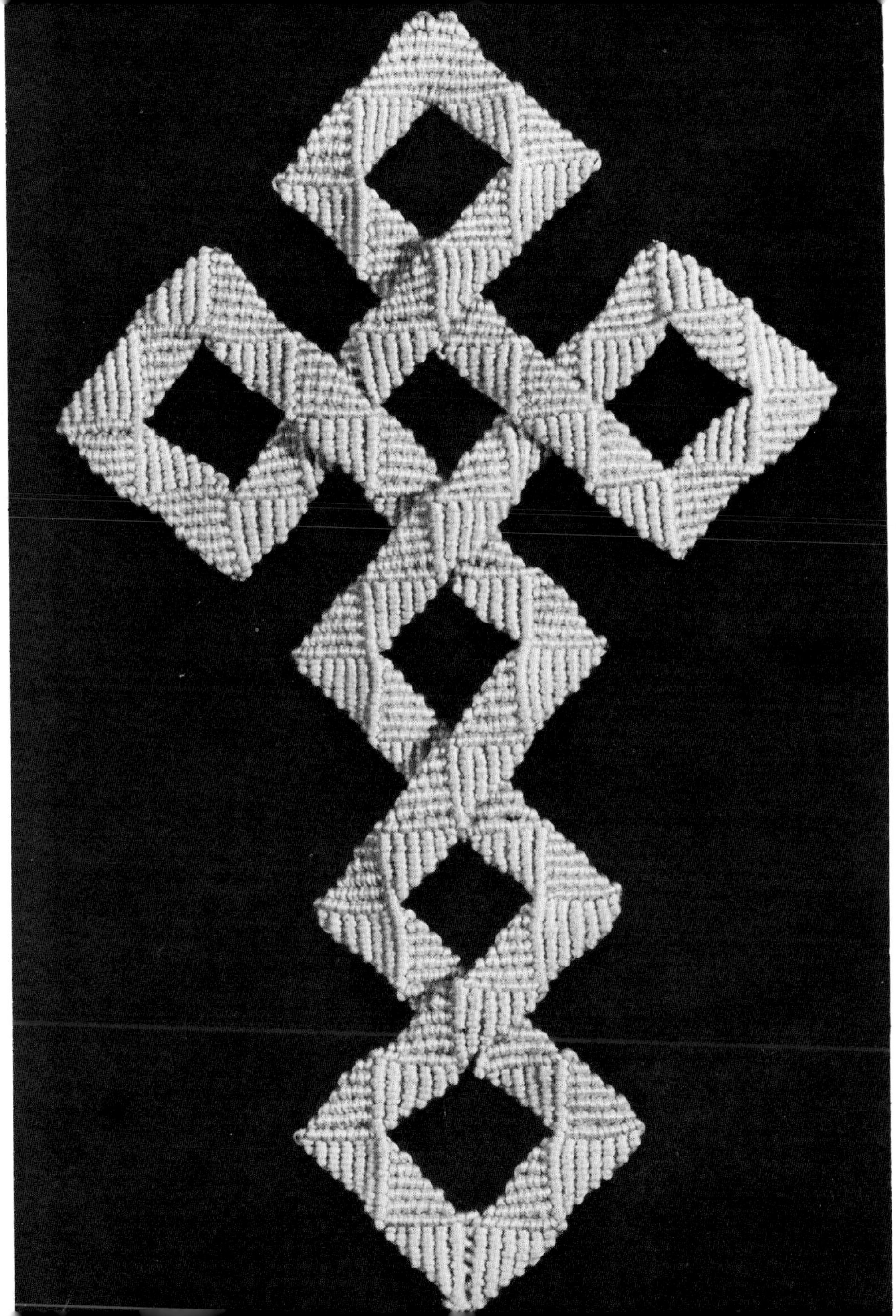

3-66

3-66. The author knotted this cross with linen shoe- stitching twine.

3-67

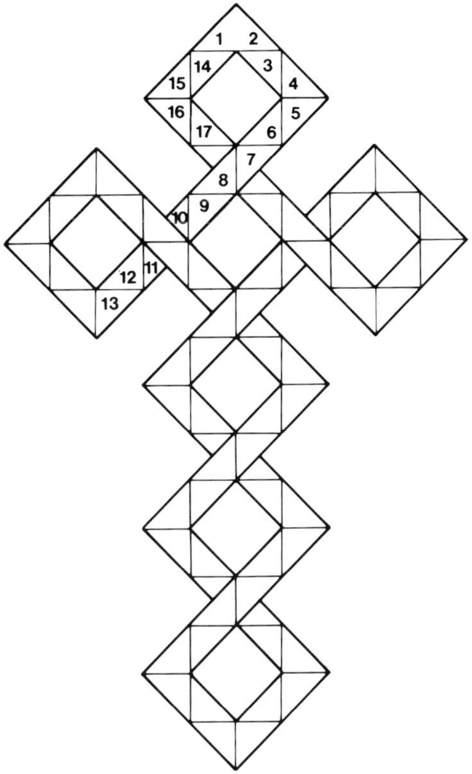

3-67. Dimensions: approximately 4″ x 7½″.

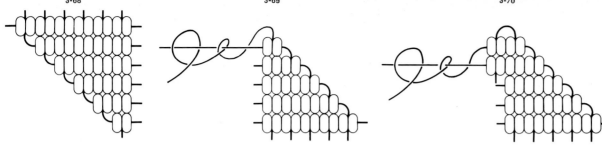
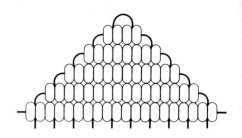

The cross was started by knotting a triangle that moves to the right.

Then the work is turned a one-half turn and a triangle is knotted starting with one knot beside the single knot that was the last one of the previous triangle.

The two cords used for the first knot are knotted on the cord immediately below it.

Each successive row is one knot wider because the holding cord of the previous row is added to the knotting cords. When the rows are completed, the form becomes a triangle twice the size of the original one.

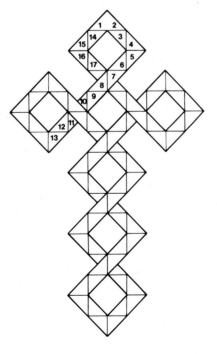

After having followed instructions for triangles 1 and 2 as explained above, the following outline should then be followed for successive triangles:

3. The holding cord comes from the right-angle side of 2, and it is held in the right hand.
4. The holding cord comes from the point of 4, and it is held in the left hand.
5. The holding cord comes from the point of 4, and it is held in the left hand.
6. The holding cord comes from the right-angle side of 5, and it is held in the right hand. Continue taking from the right-angle side until 13 is completed, and then repeat 5.

Then triangles 14, 15, 16, and 17 are knotted:
14. Holding cord from right-angle of 1 in left hand.
15. Holding cord from right angle of 14 in right hand.
16. Holding cord from point of 15 in right hand.
17. Holding cord from right angle of 16 in left hand.

Follow the triangles as they are marked on the design to complete the cross.
The two knotted sections come together at the center bottom, where they were knotted together and the ends clipped short on the reverse side.

The Diagonal Double Half Hitch can be used in a circular motif. Starting with a horizontal row, turn the holding cord and knot a diagonal. Again, turn the holding cord and knot a second row immediately below and adjacent to the last row. These two rows become the first spoke of a wheel form in which each spoke is a duplicate of the last two rows of knotting and lies at a 45° angle to the previous spoke. The solid lines indicate rows of Double Half Hitches. Continuing the same sequence of spokes, a full circle is formed.

Reversing the direction of the spokes after a half circle has been knotted will give the form an undulating flow.

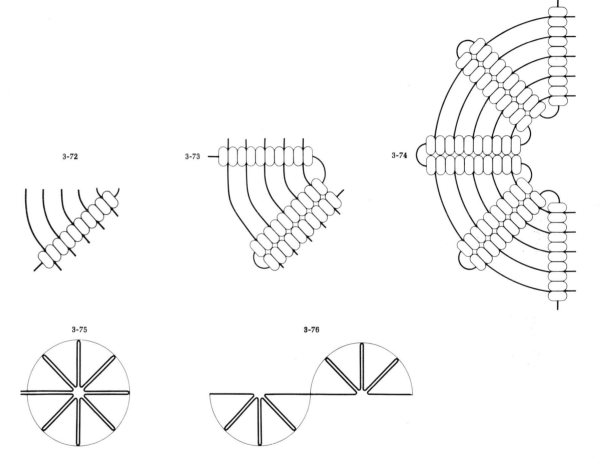

3-72

3-73

3-74

3-75

3-76

These simplified line forms can be used as a shorthand device in sketching, or they can be drawn, cut out, and used for designing.

One quarter of the wheel can be
used to form a handsome braid.

3-78

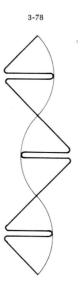

3-79

3-79. The wheel with the ends gathered to form a tassel becomes
a coaster. This was a quick project knotted of rayon satin cord
by the author.

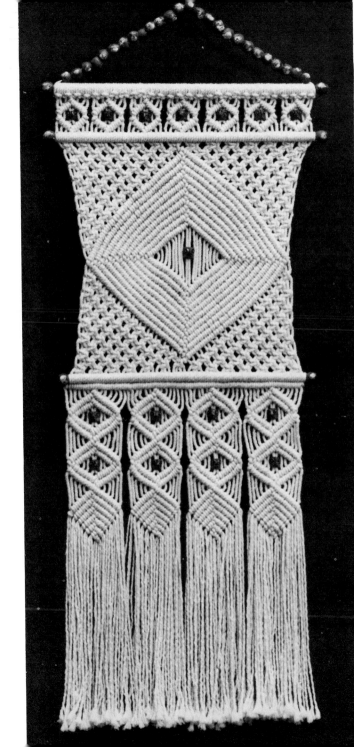

Designing with Diamond Motifs

One of the structural qualities of a large part of knotted design is the diagonal line, and so it is natural that many of the patterns are built on the diamond form. In Fig. 3-80 Carol Robinson has emphasized the diamond motif and repeated it in a wall hanging. The simplicity of the form enhances the beauty of the hanging.

The diamond forms softened by the curved lines surrounding them make a handsome design on a pottery jar in this work by Joan Michaels Paque (Fig. 3-81).

3-80

3-81

3-80. (Photograph by Lincoln Potter.)

3-81. (Photograph by Joan Michaels Paque.)

3-82

Diamonds are formed by the grid pattern discussed on page 30. When the diamonds are enlarged, a pattern can be introduced into them, as shown at left. (From *Macramé: The Art of Creative Knotting* by Virginia I. Harvey, Reinhold, 1967.) If the diamond motifs are separated, the diagonals of the pattern are not so insistent. The pattern at the left is a detail from the shoulder bag of cotton seine twine shown at the right. The bag, which was purchased in Crete by Mildred Sherwood, was given to the author to add to her collection of macramé.

3-83

3-84

The diamonds can be enclosed by bands of knotted pattern.

3-85. A natural linen stitching twine combined with Elm Flax, a waxed linen upholsterer's cord.

3-86. Two colors of cotton Belfast cord combined in a diamond pattern.

3-85

3-86

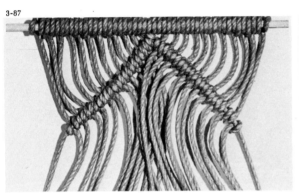

3-87

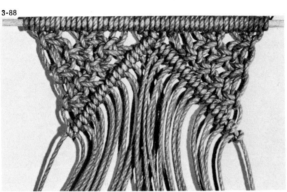

3-88

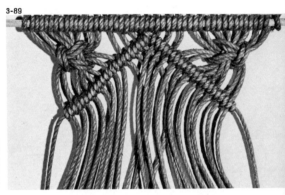

3-89

When the knotting begins at a horizontal line, it is necessary to move from a horizontal to a diagonal line before a diamond pattern can begin. There are many ways to fill this triangular space. The knotting can move directly from horizontal to diagonal with no pattern in between except the soft curve of the cords —

The space can be filled with Square Knots —

One large Square Knot, or Gathering Knot as it is sometimes called, can be used —

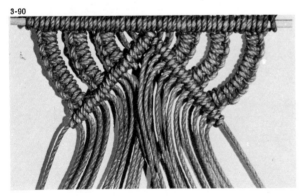

3-90

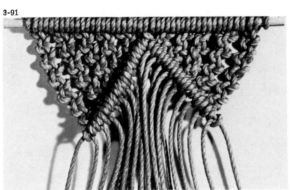

3-91

A series of Reversed Double Half Hitches will fill the space —

Or a series of chains fills the space with a rough-textured surface.

The motifs on the previous pages can be expanded to fill the spaces in a design of repeated diamonds. Across the top, where the horizontal line must be changed to a series of triangles, the right and left corners are the same as the motifs illustrated in the previous pages. In the center, the triangles must expand to double the width, and along the center sides of the pattern, larger triangles are necessary. The small knotted piece on the left illustrates the way several of the patterns look when they have been expanded and also how they can be increased further to fit the center of the diamond, but these are only a few of the many, many designs that can be used with triangular and diamond patterns. Some further discussion of designing with diamonds will be found in the next chapter.

4. COLOR

In macramé color can be combined in many ways, and some of these ways are very simple while others are more complex. Perhaps the simplest course is to use only one color in the knotted structure and introduce color in beads or other objects in the design. Within these limitations, the success of a design depends upon the knotted pattern, the color relationships of the cords and other materials that are introduced, and the unity achieved in combining all of these elements. For instance, the orange beads in Mary Stevens Nelson's tan linen hanging give it life and sparkle (Fig. 4-1). Another good example are the beads of several colors that have been introduced into the necklace with the circular medallion. (See Fig. C-34.) Dark green tensolite served as a background for beads ranging in color from blue through olive green into antique gold.

Another of the easier ways of controlling color is by knotting groups of the same colored cords together and then overlaying or intertwining them with a knotted group of another color to form the desired design. (See Fig. C-30.) Thus the separate colors are not knotted together, but they move from one position to another and combine into a multicolored composition. (See Figs. C-31 and C-32.) The overlays can be knotted with any of the knots found in macramé. The Double Half Hitch moves in a solid, simple form, either right, left, or vertically, and it will form an angle when necessary. Any of the sinnets made with the Square Knot, the Double Half Hitch, the Reversed Double Half Hitch, the Overhand Knot, or the Josephine Knot will overlay, underlay, and intertwine horizontally, vertically, diagonally, or in a curved line when the design demands it. (See Figs. 1-4, p. 8, and C-24.)

Designing with color within the knotted structure itself, whether in layers as described above or in an integrated design, requires a thorough knowledge of the various ways the colors combine in each of the individual knots and how colors move in a knotted structure.

All of the knots we will discuss are tied with either two or four cords. In the knots tied with two cords, such as the Double Half Hitch and the Overhand Knot, one cord is hidden and the other cord shows (except when both cords move as one in the Overhand Knot). When two colors are used for these knots, it is possible to create an infinite number of patterns, and when you add two more cords and knot a Square Knot or a Double Chain, you add several more possible combinations.

Although the principles of color manipulation are simple, the many possible variations make the subject complex. The theory of color movement can be understood from reading a discussion of it, but it is necessary to apply the theory before it becomes a useful tool to the knotter.

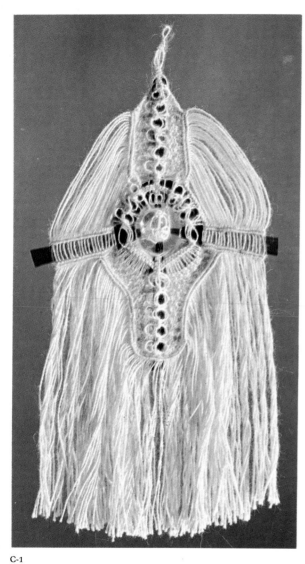

C-1

C-1. In Paul A. Johnson's handsome design, made of white yarn combined with lucite strips and a transparent sphere, the areas of knotted pattern contrast with the unknotted sections in such a way that the characteristics of the materials are enhanced.

C-2

C-2. Detail of C-1.

C-3. Glen Kaufman has skillfully combined linen, beads, wood, and guinea fowl feathers in "The Red Fan." The playful, three-dimensional piece stands 25″ high when extended. (Photograph by Glen Kaufman.)

C-4. Detail of C-3. (Photograph by Glen Kaufman.)

C-5. Anne Hawkins' belt of rayon satin cord features an orderly progression of rich colors in the side section that contrasts with a different distribution of the same colors in the center part.

C-6a. Modified diamond motifs in a light and dark tone of the same color of rayon satin cord make a handsome accessory as knotted by Mary Sayler.

C-6b. A definite change of color emphasis has been achieved in this belt by Anne Hawkins by using the red satin cord for a holding cord in the upper section, then shifting to tan holding cords in the lower section.

C-6c. Jute yarn in muted colors and a simple diamond design by Anne Hawkins.

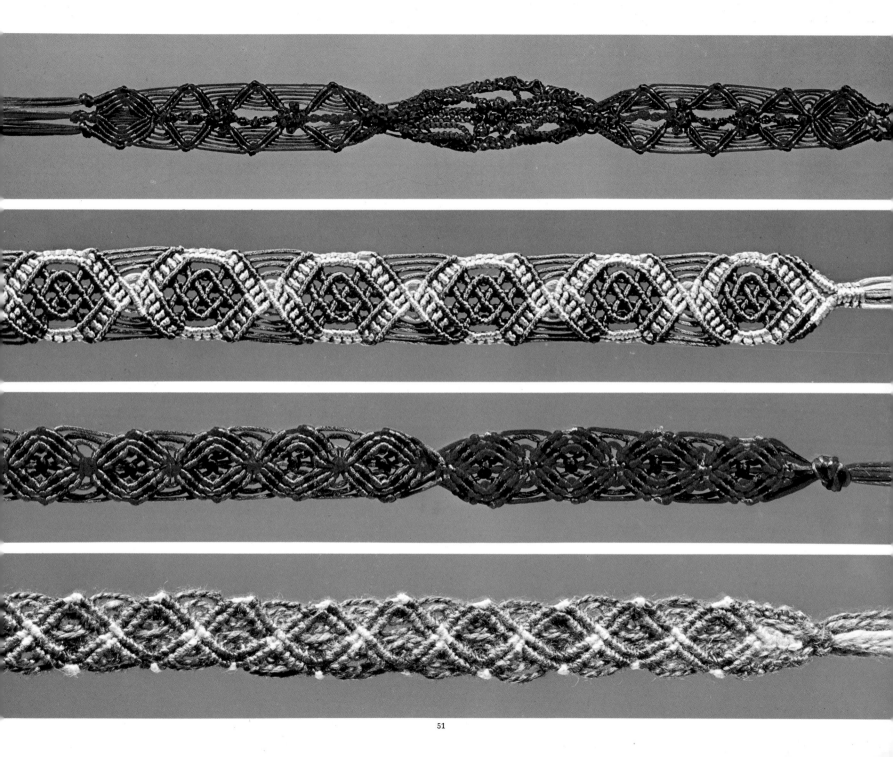

51

C-7. This ceremonial plate by
Ed Rossbach is purely decorative.
Skillful shaping and color
manipulation combine to make
an object that has interesting
dimension, warm low-keyed
color, and an unusual design.

C-8. Ed Rossbach has produced
a magnificent knotted statement
in which he has controlled the
color so skillfully that it appears
and disappears throughout the
piece with ease and freedom.
(Shown by courtesy of the Art
Museum, Indiana University.)

C-8

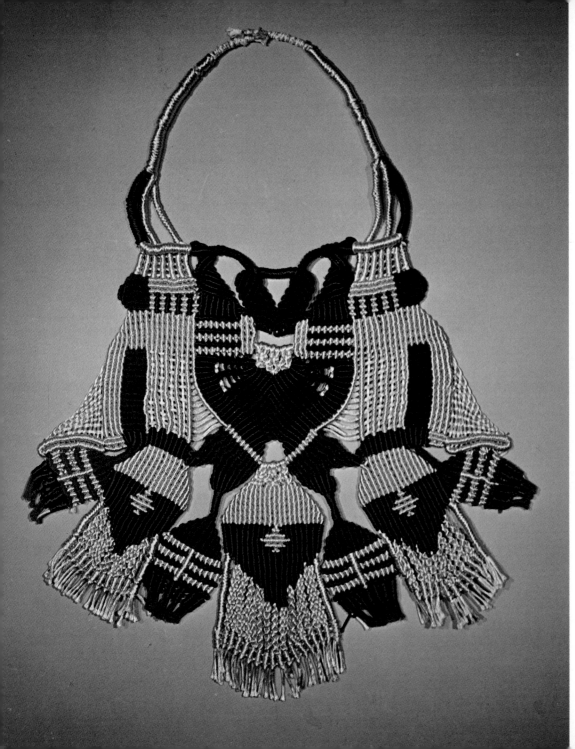

C-9. This body ornament that fastens around the neck was created by Helen Bitar. Satin cord (rayon) has been knotted with very skillful color control. (Photograph by William Eng.)

C-10. Helen Bitar has knotted a small wall hanging of wool (approximately 9″ at the widest section) with areas of contrasting colors that have been isolated to emphasize the design.

C-11. Rich, warm colors in cotton mat-finished embroidery floss have been knotted by Helen Bitar with remarkable color control to create this small wall hanging that is approximately 12″ at its widest part.

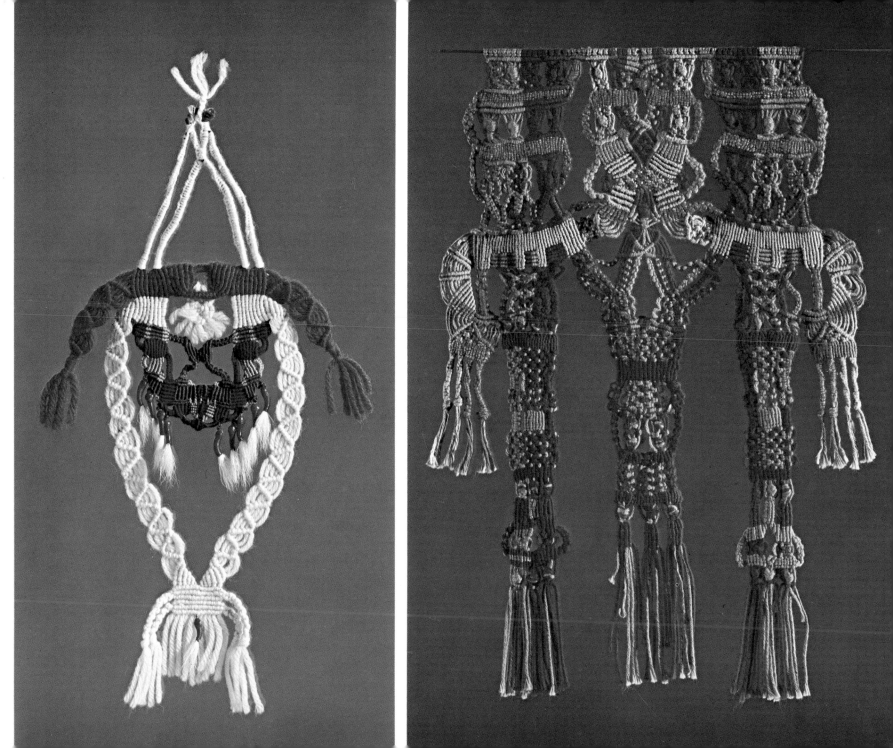

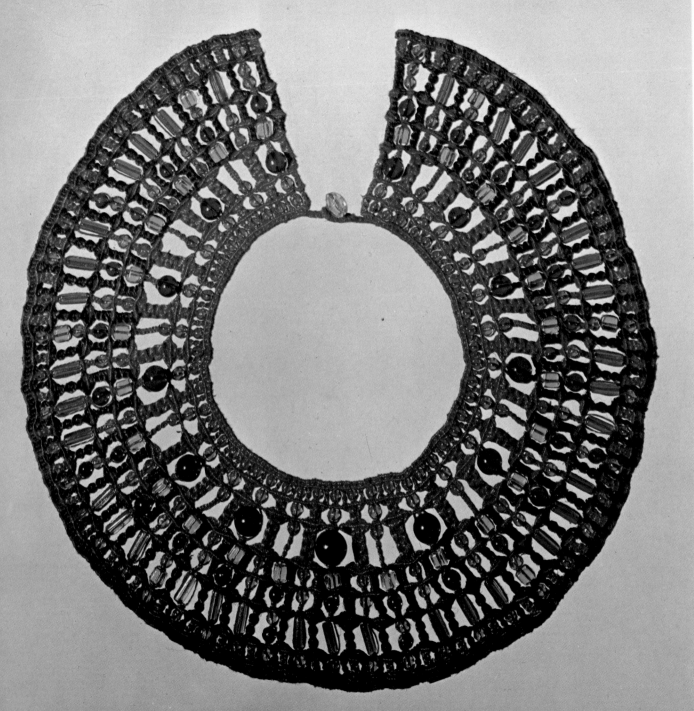

C-12. Larry Edman has used antique beads held in a framework of knotted 10 lea, 2-ply linen to form a very decorative collar that is 14″ across.

C-13. This small tapestry with colors intermingled in an abstract design was knotted by Ron Franks.

C-14. A rich blend of blues and greens in a variety of materials have been combined by Gervaise Livingston in a circular hanging. Yarns were mounted on a hoop to begin the work. Feathers add interest and beads add weight to the ends of the yarns.
(Photograph by Robert Lopez.)

C-15. This large hanging, bold in its color and design, uses the diamond motif as a theme. Knotted by Mary Stephens Nelson of rug wool, it is notable for its interesting treatment at the beginning, at the bottom edge, and the illusion of framing given by the two long blue pieces at the sides.

C-16. Detail of C-15.

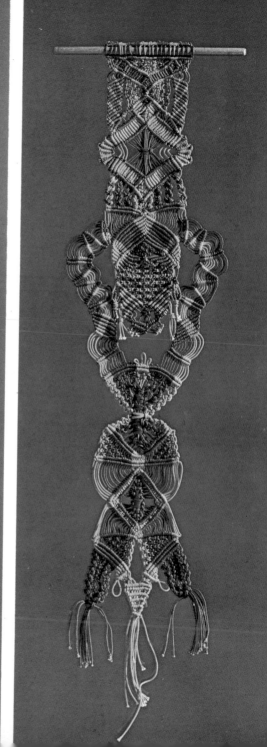

C-17. Two colors of yarn have
been controlled very carefully to
produce this eight-pointed star
knotted by Mary Stephens
Nelson. Diameter: approx-
imately 15″

C-18. This small hanging knotted
by Mary Stephens Nelson
includes an unusual mounting,
a very novel manipulation of
cords and colors, and a well-
integrated combination of
angular and circular forms.

C-19. A small, colorful hanging of
polished cotton cord knotted by
the author.

C-20. This monumental hanging of various materials, including some rope, was knotted by Francoise Grossen. (C-20 through C-22 photographed by Ferdinand Boesch.)

C-21. Detail of C-20.

C-21

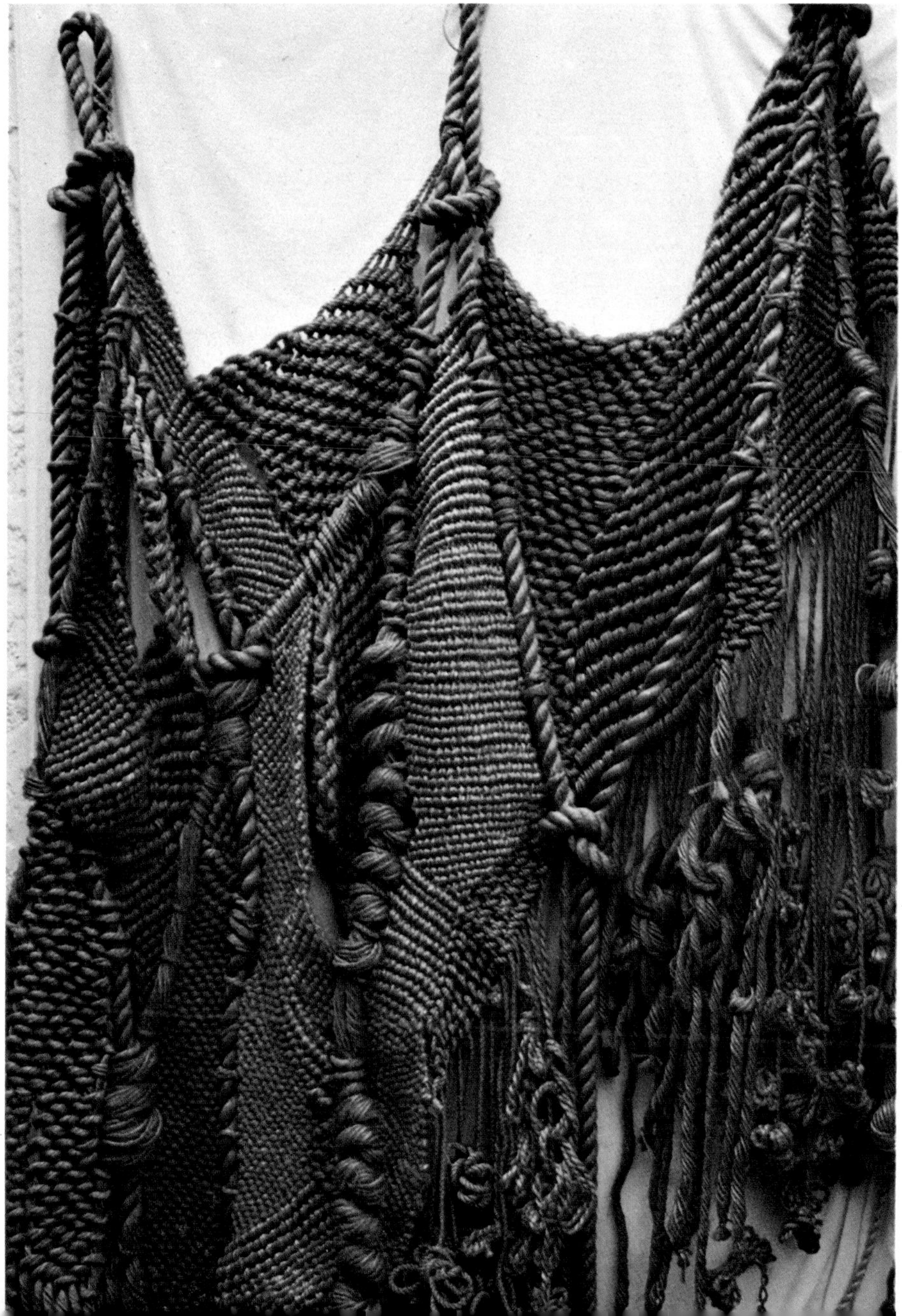

C-22

C-22. Detail of C-20.

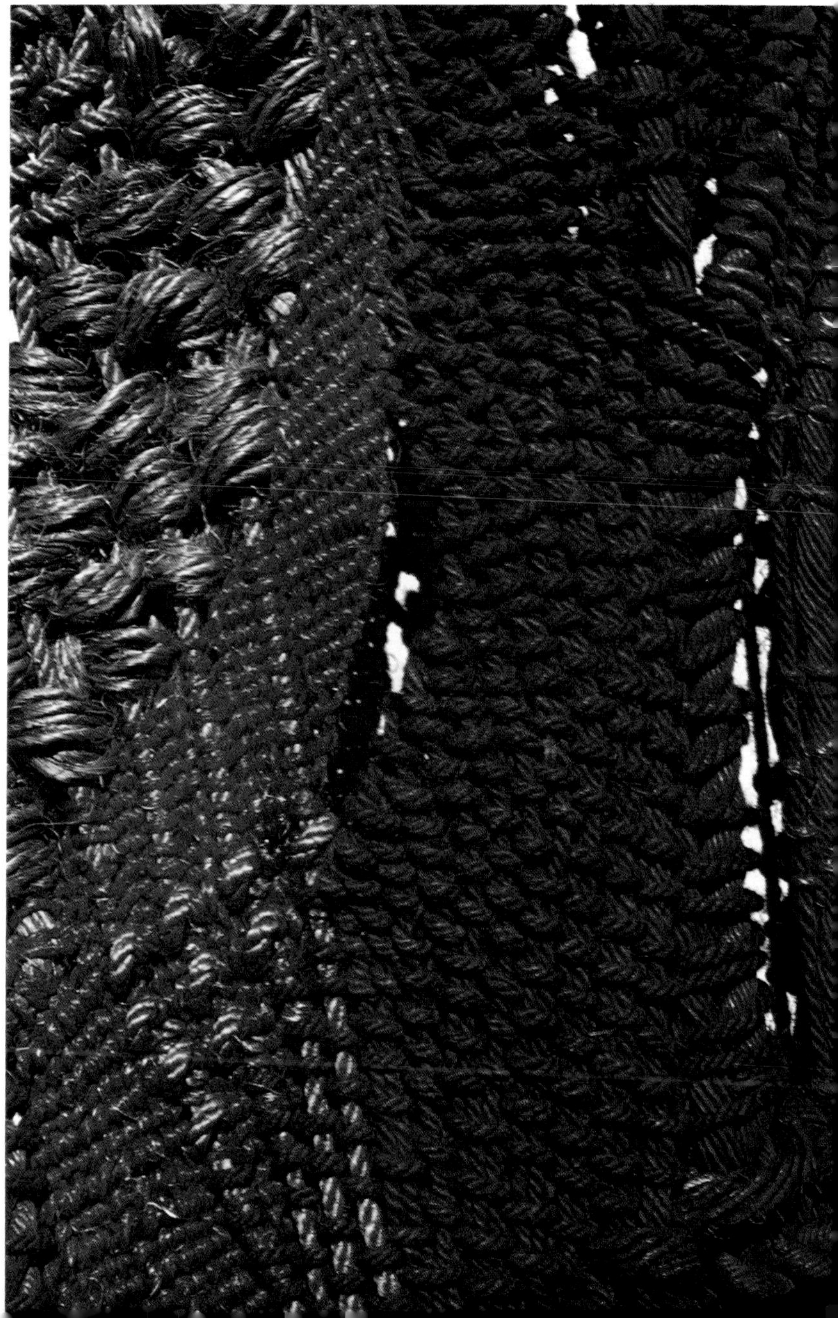

C-23

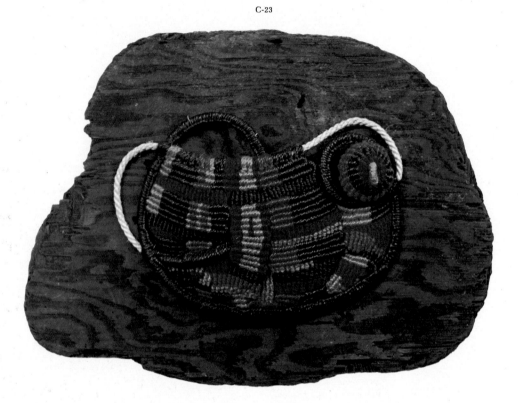

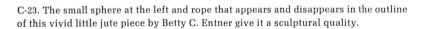

C-23. The small sphere at the left and rope that appears and disappears in the outline of this vivid little jute piece by Betty C. Entner give it a sculptural quality.

C-24. A metal choker ring was used as a base for this colorful necklace. Using three colors of rayon chainette and wood and glass beads, the author designed the necklace as she knotted it.

C-25. This pattern of circles in diamonds was knotted by the author with celtigale, a rayon yarn.

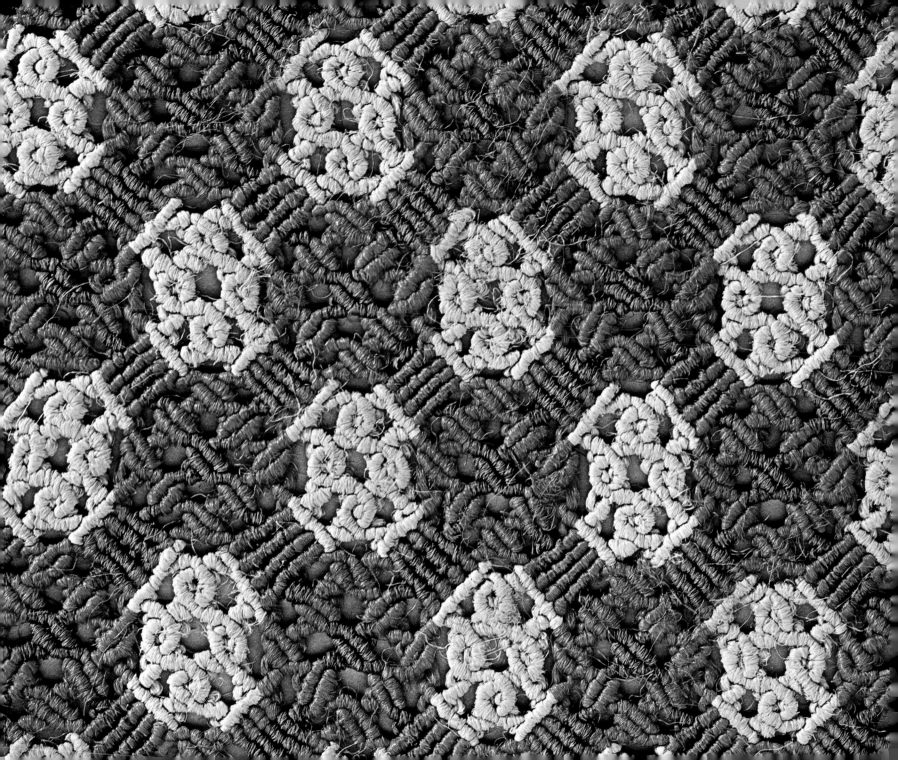

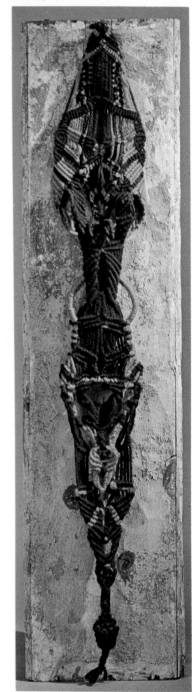

C-26. Analogous colors of rug wool, a bold design, and technical manipulation have been combined by Mary Stephens Nelson in a handsome hanging. The color in the diamond and rectangular motifs was achieved with added cords.

C-27. This sculptural hanging by Gervaise Livingston demonstrates skillful arrangement of color. (Photograph by Robert Lopez.)

C-28. Vertical Double Half Hitches in many colors and fibers are knotted over the orange silk yarns that are the predominant color of this hanging by the author.

C-29. In this fey little surrealistic
creature that will hang against
a wall or suspended in space,
Lucy Driver has capitalized on
the stiff quality of the sisal to
add humor and dimension to the
sculptural form. (Photograph by
Paul Macapia.)

C-30. A very decorative belt
knotted by Martha Ehlers in
which she has combined unusual
color in a very complex pattern
to make this stunning fashion
accessory. (Photograph by
William Eng.)

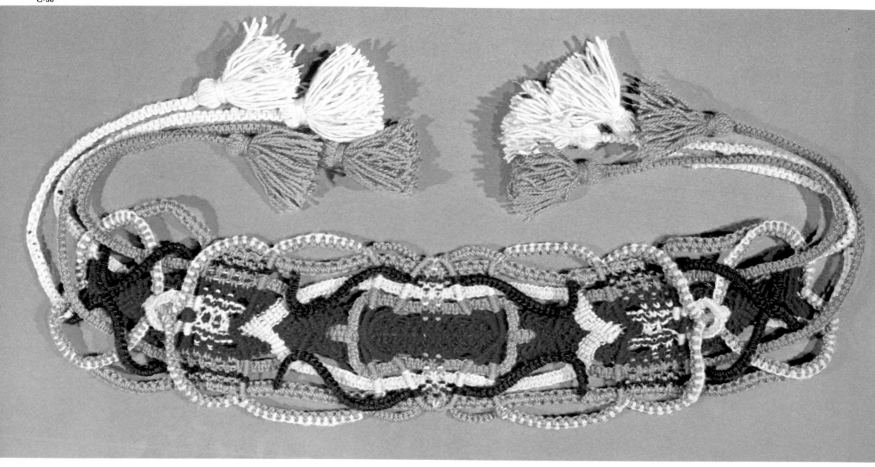

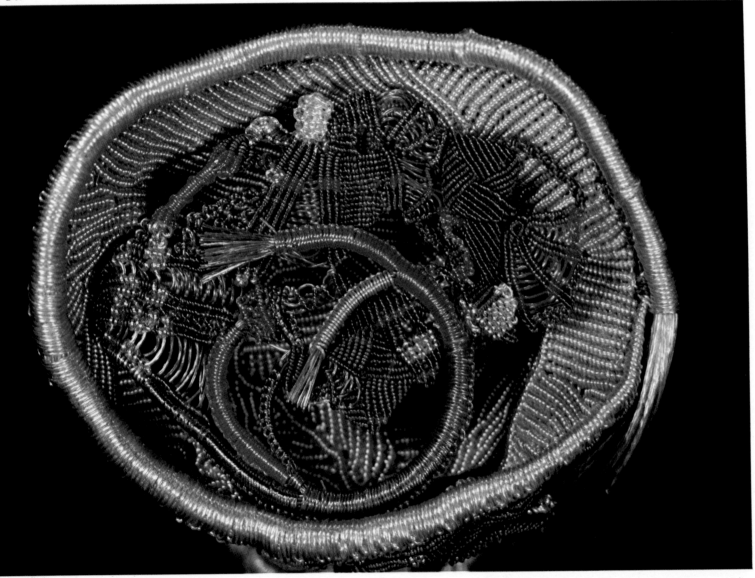

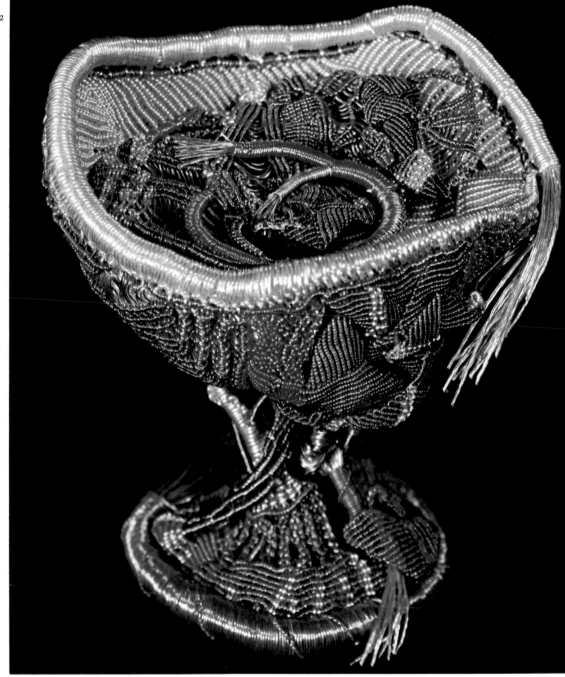

C-31 and C-32. This small piece is knotted of tensolite, a plastic cord. With its goblet-shaped container that was created as an environment for it (C-32), "The Frail Grail" forms a small table sculpture that is about 5″ high. (Photographs by Paul Macapia.)

C-33

C-34

C-35

C-33. Gervaise Livingston has combined a hoop, beads, bone rings, wool yarns, and feathers into a hanging that could be suspended in midair or hung against a wall. (Photograph by Robert Lopez.)

C-34. In this necklace knotted by the author, tensolite, a fine plastic yarn, was used as a background for wood and glass beads.

C-35. Amber-glass chandelier drops and beads and reconstituted amber beads have been combined with rayon chainette in a necklace by the author. (Photograph by William Eng.)

4-1. Tan linen and orange beads have been combined in an elegantly simple design by Mary Stephens Nelson. Dimensions: Approximately 6' x 15".

4-2. Detail of 4-1.

4-1

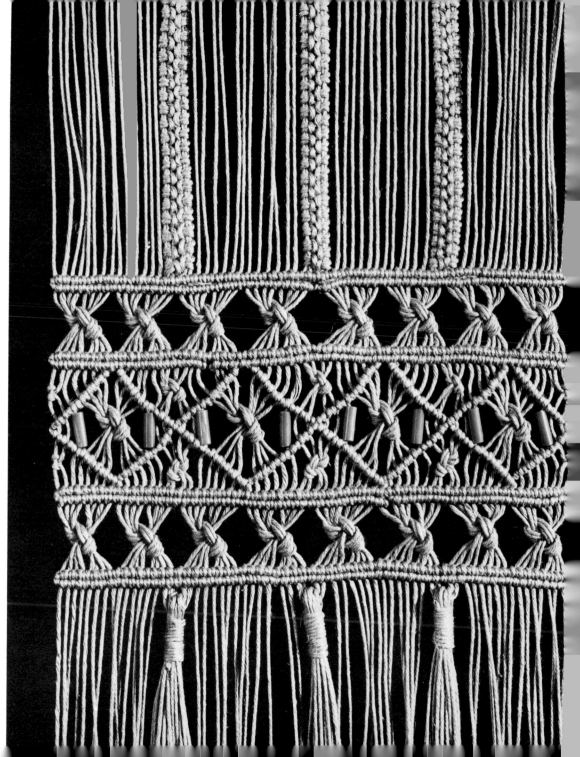

4-2

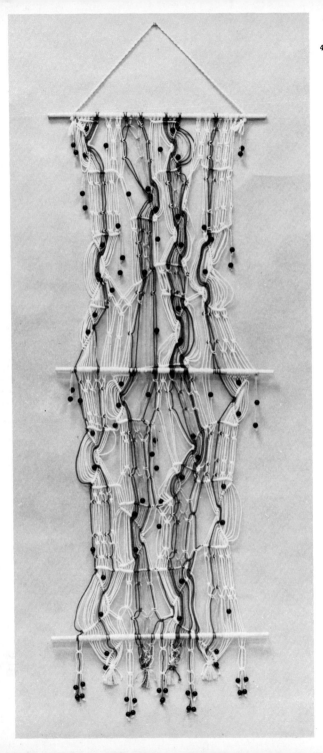

4-3. Deborah Holt Morgan has distributed beads throughout her knotting to bring in color in addition to the few colored cords which wander haphazardly through the hanging. This open piece with its casual design would be most effective as a room divider or a screen, and very interesting as a large screen if the same nonrepeating design were expanded to cover a large area. (Photograph by Al Cornette.)

4-4. A natural jute cord has been fashioned into a colorful necklace that is interesting viewed from either the front or the back. When it is not being worn, it is a handsome spot of color on a wall, where it can be hung over two nails. The piece, which was knotted by Anne Hawkins, depends entirely for its color upon the beads in various shades of orange.

Color with the Half Knot and the Square Knot

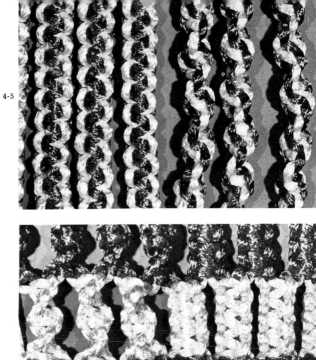

4-5

When color is used in the Half Knot and the Square Knot, it can be distributed in two different ways. First, each of the knotting cords can be a different color.

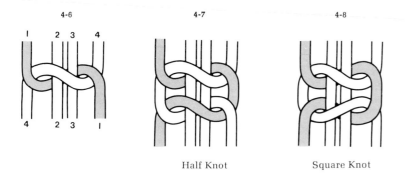

4-6 4-7 4-8

Half Knot Square Knot

4-9

Second, the knotting cords can be one color and the core cords a second color. Alternating the knots so the core cords become the knotting cords brings a change of color.
Alternating the knots in each row creates horizontal stripes of color.

4-10

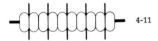 4-11

If light knotting cords are knotted over a dark holding cord, the dark cord is hidden.

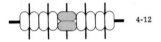 4-12

To bring the dark color to the surface, the holding cord becomes the knotting cord for a Vertical Double Half Hitch.

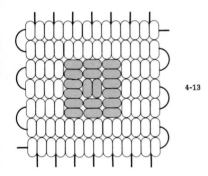 4-13

This is the basic principle used in a large part of macramé with more than one color, and whether the cords are being knotted in a horizontal, vertical, or diagonal direction, the same principle holds true. Sometimes solid knotting using Horizontal and Vertical Double Half Hitches is called Cavandoli Work.

Some of the most obvious examples of this principle can be found in color photographs 11, 16, 17, 18, and 19. Color is carried in diagonal lines through the pattern of circles and diamonds in Fig. C-25, and through the examples of patterns with diamonds in Fig. 3-85. This principle of color distribution is used very frequently in pattern repeats, but there are also many possible variations within the general theory.

4-14. Two colors of Belfast cord were used to knot the small design in Fig. 4-13.

4-15. It is easy to trace the colors as they move through this hanging by Mary Stephens Nelson.

4-16. Detail of 4-15.

4-17. Black moves through white in a casual, relaxed manner. Hanny Korringa has used Double Half Hitches horizontally, diagonally, and vertically to control the flow of the color in this small hanging which measures approximately 12″ x 26″.

Sometimes color changes are made by carrying extra colors behind the knotting, in order to substitute them where the design calls for a change. The Greek key design in the center of the hanging on the left may have been knotted this way. Also, the center part of the hanging in Fig. C-26 was knotted by substituting colors whenever necessary.

4-18. A small blue and white hanging with a variety of knotting by Judy Seiler.

Color in Chains

4-20

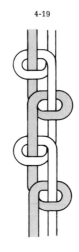

4-19

4-19. A chain in two colors.

4-21

4-22

Combining color in chains gives a salt-and-pepper or tweedy effect if there is very much value contrast in the colors used. In Fig. 4-20, the four chains on the left side were knotted very firmly, the four in the middle with moderate tension, and the group at the right were looped with little tension.

Horizontal bands of mixed colors are alternated with bands of solid dark and solid light chains when the pairs of cords forming the knots are changed.

Double Chains are knotted with four cords, so that there are four possible combinations with two colors:

Two dark cords knotted with two light cords.

One dark and one light cord knotted with one dark and one light cord.

One dark and one light cord knotted with two dark cords.

One dark and one light cord knotted with two light cords.

The Overhand Knot can be used to mix colors or to isolate them, depending upon the way it is tied.

When two cords of different colors are tied together, then the colors are mixed as in Fig. 4-23.

4-23

When one cord is tied over the other, the color of the one looped over will show. If the knots are kept next to each other, only the knots will show, so the design will dictate which cord is tied over which. For the best effect, the cords should remain in their relative positions, with the knot being tied with either the right or left hand, depending upon which is necessary to produce the knot with the correct color.

4-24	**4-25**	**4-26**	**4-27**

4-24. Tied with the right hand.	4-25. Tied with the left hand.	4-26. Tied with the right hand.	4-27. Tied with the left hand.

The Reversed Double Half Hitch is usually tied so the core cords are covered, and there is no intermixing of colors within the knot. Cords of different color are carried through the work and interwoven or interlaced and thus the colors are controlled in the desired way, but the knot is used to hold them together rather than to mix the color. Handsome braids can be knotted in color with the Reversed Double Half Hitch. When knotted in a progression from light to dark, four colors are interesting, as seen in Fig. 4-29.

4-28. A pattern in two colors of satin cord knotted with the Overhand Knot.

4-29. All of these braids were knotted with rayon satin cord. The three on the left were knotted on the core with Reversed Double Half Hitches, while the braid at the right was knotted with Double Half Hitches.

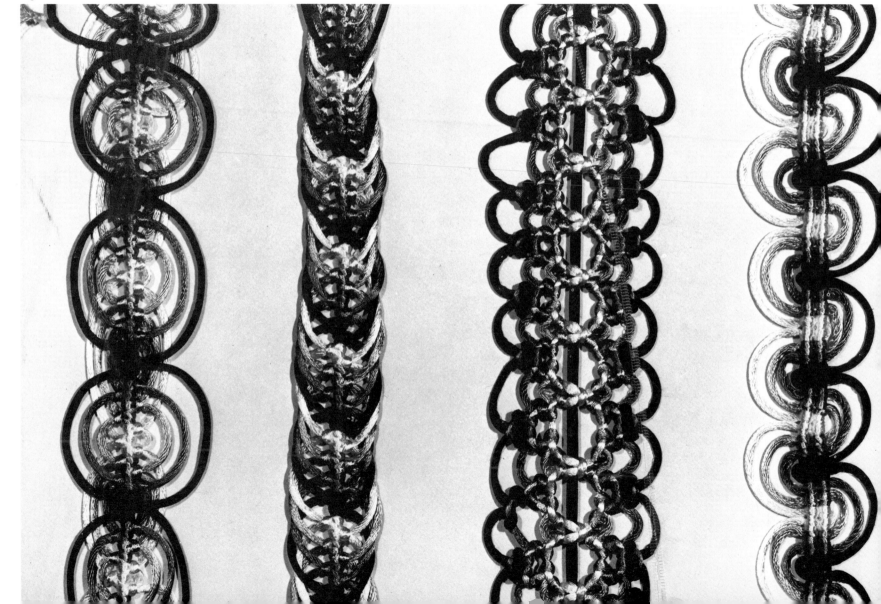

Applications of the principles just discussed can be found in the knots and the color manipulation within the structures of the pieces shown in the color illustrations.

Color alone can be a lifetime study, so any information on general color theory should be sought from publications on that subject. However, there are a few additional principles that are helpful to keep in mind when designing macramé.

As mentioned earlier, texture is a very important quality of macramé, and texture in knotting depends upon the shadow patterns created by the knots. If a textured area in a knotting is to be viewed at a distance, the color of the knotting material should be light enough to show contrast between the yarn and the shadows. A textured surface in a dark color can create a rich, luxurious effect when viewed at close range, but the quality of the textured surface will be lost at a distance.

The warm and cool qualities of color are important for creating dimension. A warm color advances and a cool color recedes, so a bright orange circle in a field of blue would give the impression that the circle is nearer than its background. In knotting, these qualities can be made to work for the designer if he is aware of them as he plans his macramé designs.

The explanations in this chapter should make for an awareness of how color is controlled in the knots themselves. Taking this knowledge and applying it to the information in Chapter 3 on how the knots combine to make pattern should provide a basis for color experimentation that will help the knotter understand how to design with color. Color control in macramé is complex, and the patterns that are possible and the variations that can be devised endless. This fascinating aspect of the craft is one that every knotter should explore so it becomes a part of his knowledge of the technique — for his own pleasure and to bring more depth and excitement to his creations.

5. THE THIRD DIMENSION

Moving into a third dimension with macramé is not complex, and there are so many ways it can be achieved that it is difficult to choose the ones to cover in a limited discussion. For instance, there is the amount or scale of the dimension desired, for the cord itself has depth, and tying it in a knot gives the work even more depth.

5-2

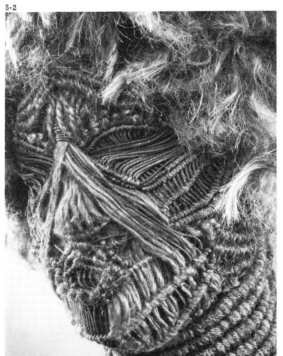

5-1. A human form in macramé by Linda R. Abbott, whose rare talent in sculpture has formed this lifelike bust of several materials. (Photograph by John Gebhart.)

5-2. Detail of 5-1. (Photograph by John Gebhart.)

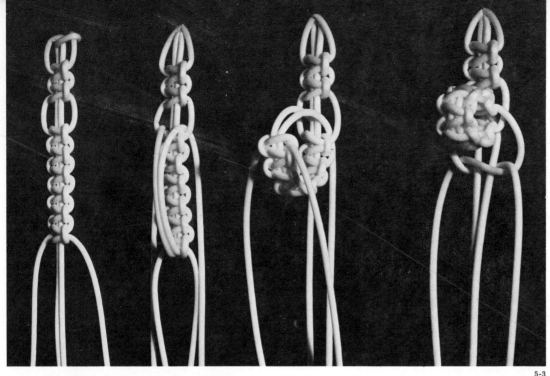

5-3

5-4. This photograph of the popcorn stitch in a deep fringe comes from *Sylvia's Book of Macramé Lace*, ca. 1882–1885. (No author and publisher are given in the book.)

5-5. Diagonals are knotted from the two center cords.

5-6. One Square Knot is tied under each diagonal.

5-7. The four cords on the right become holding cords and the four cords on the left knot four rows of Double Half Hitches over them.

5-4

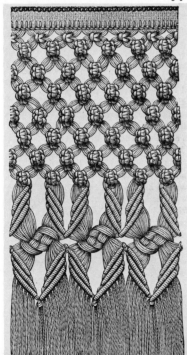

If a small degree of depth is desired, the popcorn stitch, which is a sinnet of Square Knots circled and tied back into itself, will bring the surface forward. (See Fig. 5-3.)
The button form will do the same thing. (See Figs. 5-5 to 5-10.)

5-5

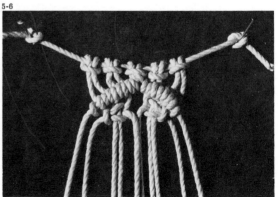

5-6

5-8. One Square Knot is tied in the right-hand group of cords and another in the left-hand group. These two knots must be tied very firmly.

5-9. The two diagonals are completed so they frame the button form by bringing the former holding cord hanging at the left around under the button and knotting the four cords from the Square Knot on it. The four cords on the right are knotted on the right-hand holding cord, and finally the holding cord from the left is knotted over the holding cord from the right to complete the button form.

5-10. This Hobnail Pattern, which features the button, was knotted of white nylon upholsterer's cord.

5-10

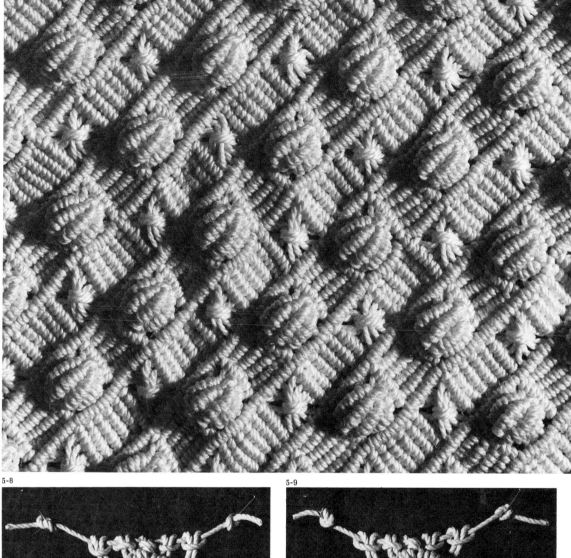

5-7

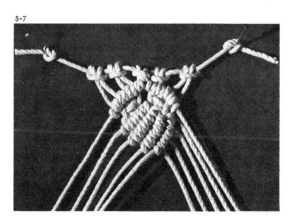

5-8

5-9

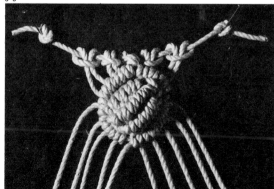

5-11

5-12

5-13 Rounded columns can be knotted over a core of many cords. One loop of the Double Half Hitch gives a smooth column with a spiral line where the cords cross. (See Fig. 5-11.)

The Reversed Double Half Hitch makes a handsome covering on a heavy cord, and it can be formed in graceful curves. (See Fig. 5-12.)

Two Half-Knot sinnets will combine into a handsome column. (See Fig. 5-13.)

A simple line, either curved or straight, can be created so it lifts off the surface of the knotting by wrapping over a heavy cord or a core of several cords. The texture of the wrapped surface is very sympathetic with knotted pattern.

The surface of the knotting can be turned or twisted and then brought back into the work as in Fig. 5-17.

The stiffness of some cords makes it possible to mold the knotting into a sculptural form with dimension. (See Fig. 5-18.)

5-15

5-14

5-16

5-14. Carol Robinson has used many cords wrapped firmly to give dimension and to add drama to her hanging. (Photograph by Lincoln Potter.)

5-15. Sharon Amii Mills' three-dimensional form is a mixture of materials that features groups of cords wrapped very firmly. (Photograph by Robert Lopez.)

5-16. Detail of 5-15. (Photograph by Robert Lopez.)

5-17. Rayon chainette, knotted by the author.

5-18. A white sculptural form that stands about four feet high, this piece was knotted of several plastic cords by Robert Mills. (5-18 to 5-20 photographed by Robert Lopez.)

5-19. Detail of 5-18.

5-20. Detail of 5-18.

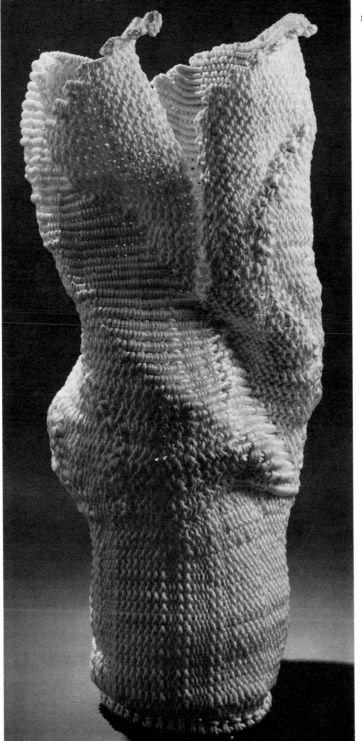

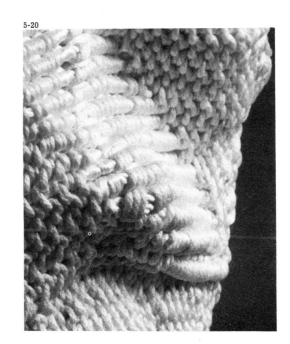

5-21. Joan Michaels Paque has combined knotting and looping in a space hanging of red, pumpkin, orange, and gold jute. (Photograph by Joan Michaels Paque.)

5-22. "Ode to a Bicycle Thief" by Polly Goodman is knotted of natural linen and is 8′ high and 36″ wide.

5-23. A metal cube forms the structure on which Ron Franks has knotted this unusual sculpture. Knotting moves within the cube as well as around it. (Photograph by Darrell Muething.)

5-23

Many cords brought together and knotted over will create a form that is stiff enough to hold a shape, as shown in Figs. C-31 and C-32. Usually the knotter is interested in dimension as it refers to free-hanging forms and sculptural pieces, and one of the simplest and most direct ways of creating a three-dimensional form is by starting the knotting on a wire or wood hoop. The knotting cords are placed directly on the hoop, and the knotting proceeds down the length of the piece. Frequently more hoops are introduced into the work as it progresses. These supports for the knotting are usually circular, but triangles, rectangles, and free-form shapes would be challenging, and any of them could form the support for an exciting sculptural shape.

Knotting within a three-dimensional form is another approach that has many possibilities and when the artist is designing within a form, he frequently thinks of the form as the environment for his work. The design must develop from that which surrounds it, with the result that the design and its container belong to each other and become a total statement, not two separate entities that happen to come together.

5-21   5-22

5-24

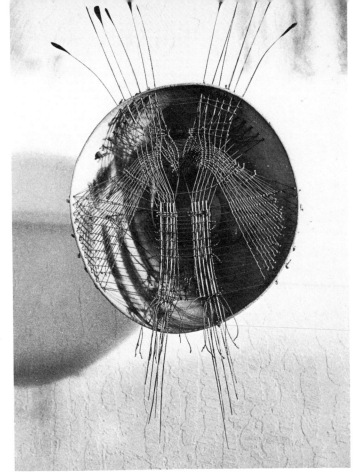

5-25
5-26

5-24. Detail of 5-23. (Photograph
by Darrell Muething.)

5-25. Delicate cords, a minimum
of knots, and feathers are
combined within a clay form by
Dominic L. DiMare. Dimensions:
6½" x 9". (Photograph by
Constance Beeson.)

5-26. This graceful, sculptural
form by Dominic L. DiMare is
made with knotting and feathers.
(Photograph by Constance
Beeson.)

5-27. The author covered a whiskey bottle with white nylon upholsterer's cord.

5-28. Detail of 5-27. The bottle was covered by starting at the neck and finishing at the bottom, with the horizontal and vertical lines that cross at the center of the bottom marking the knots where the ends were tied and then tucked into the back to conceal them.

5-29. Glen Kaufman knotted cotton cord over a Plexiglas base. Dimensions: 20″ x 7″. (Photograph by Nathan Rabin.)

Instead of knotting within a piece, a form can be used as a base for a knotted shape, such as a covering for a bottle. Covered bottles are a traditional product of seamen, and they must have been functional at one time, when they protected beautiful flasks in a heavy sea. Bottles that come in handsome or unusual shapes are challenging and exciting to cover. Other interesting forms that lend themselves well to a macramé covering are the plastic cylinders for lampshades or the Plexiglas cylinder Glen Kaufman used as a base for his sculptural piece. (See Fig. 5-29.)

It should be apparent from the foregoing that macramé can be shaped into almost any form. The designer who has a broad knowledge of all the possible combinations in the technique and an active imagination will find the variations of three-dimensional form almost limitless and within this area of the third dimension in macramé great scope for creativity and originality.

6. MORE COMBINATIONS AND CONTRASTS

It is always stimulating and beneficial for students and artists to view the works of others. Comparing designs of knotters brings out many interesting contrasts, both within some of the pieces and between the different interpretations of the technique. Within the designs, materials have been combined with skill, so that there are contrasts such as hard against soft, shiny against dull, patterned with plain, large with small, simple with complex, to name a few, in the examples shown in this chapter.

Some of the artists' interpretations have been handsome, formal arrangements. When one of these is so starkly simple as to be almost an understatement, it is an interesting contrast to a complex, formal hanging that is monumental in size. In turn, formal designs contrast with some pieces that have a soft, draping quality and others that achieve a softness from an emphasis of the softer yarn from which they are knotted.

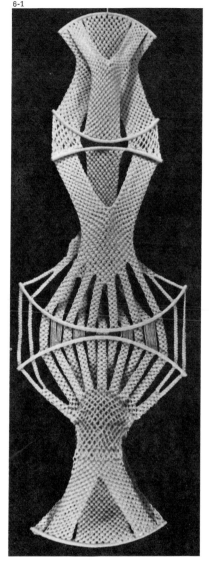

6-1

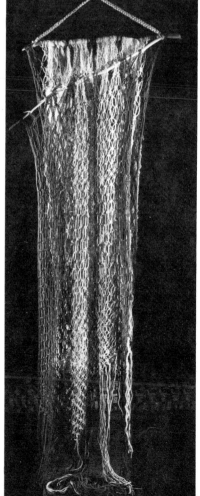

6-2. "The Nets are Empty" by Else Regensteiner consists of two knotted layers with a woven background. The background is woven in light greens and yellow shades, the center layer is dark brown rug wool, and the top layer is knotted in naturals and blacks. The materials are linen, jute, wool, horsehair, mohair, cotton, and driftwood. Dimensions: 3′ x 11′. (Photograph by John W. Rosenthal.)

6-2

6-1. Barbara J. Wittenberg's handsome layered hanging is knotted of white rayon. (Photograph by Janet Luks.)

6-3

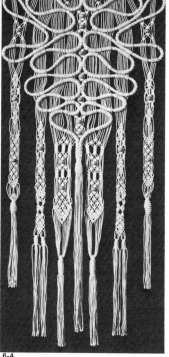

6-4

Scale acts as the most important element in Francoise Grossen's simple statement in Fig. 6-3, while Mary Stephens Nelson's hanging is more complex. (See Fig. 6-4.) Mrs. Nelson has combined her materials so that the stiffness of the rope has worked to her advantage, giving an interesting, fluid quality to the design.

Susan Wynhoff Caffrey's simple, well-designed horoscope necklaces combine a minimum of knots and a few handsome beads. (See Fig. 6-6.) They are excellent examples of skillful designing for commercial sales because she has achieved an appealing product that can be knotted quickly, and therefore it can be sold at a price that will bring the proper compensation for the time and materials.

Another design that could be knotted and sold is the simple necklace of natural linen by Margaret Windeknecht. (See Fig. 6-7.) However, the more complex jewelry by Paul Johnson, Mary Stephens Nelson, Luella Simpson, and the author would be more apt to be one-of-a-kind creations. (See Figs. 6-8 to 6-12.) The contrasts to be found among this jewelry is intriguing: the smooth rigidity of silver wire as against the airy feathers; the simplicity of some of the designs as opposed to the complex pattern of others; earthy, natural design compared to sophisticated, formal pattern; and, of course, there are contrasts among the yarn sizes — from fine through medium to heavy.

6-3. The simplicity of the fine-scaled cord Double Half Hitched over rope contributes to the beauty of this treatment of a store window by Francoise Grossen. (Photograph by Ferdinand Boesch.)

6-4. Mary Stephens Nelson has used rope as a holding cord for a smaller-sized linen cord. Dimensions: approximately 25" x 48".

6-5. Detail of 6-4.

6-6. Susan Wynhoff Caffrey has knotted horoscope necklaces with waxed linen upholsterer's cord, pottery beads, and medallions.

6-7. This simple necklace of linen carpet warp and wood beads was knotted by Margaret Winderknecht.

6-5

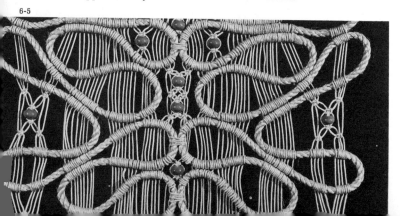

6-6

6-7

6-8

6-8. Red plastic tensolite cord has been combined with red and white glass beads from old necklaces in this piece by the author.

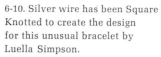

6-9. Paul Johnson has knotted a choker with a large, elaborate pendant.

6-10. Silver wire has been Square Knotted to create the design for this unusual bracelet by Luella Simpson.

6-11. Silver beads, some with Square Knotted wire and some simple cylinders, are combined with Indian shell disks in this beautiful necklace by Luella Simpson.

6-12. An unusual combination of feathers and rayon cord has been knotted into a necklace by Mary Stephens Nelson.

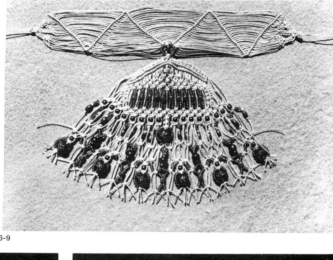

6-9

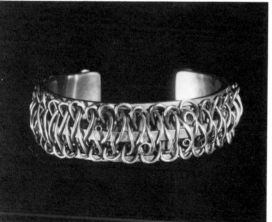

6-10

6-11

6-12

6-13. Carol Robinson has attached a circular bowl to a circular ring with Square Knotted sinnets adorned with beads. (Photograph by Lincoln Potter.)

6-14. Knotted by the author, "The Sun" is a mixture of materials in many shades of yellows and oranges. Diameter: approximately 30".

6-15. A shoulder bag by Donna Lowe.

6-16. This hanging by Carol Robinson employs pottery forms. (Photograph by Lincoln Potter.)

6-13

Circular forms can be used as a beginning for simple or complex designs. (See Figs. 6-13 and 6-14.)

The functional bag (Fig. 6-15) and the decorative hanging (Fig. 6-16) both employ contrasts of simple, uncomplicated surfaces with knotted pattern, and both pieces are excellent examples of combining materials so they complement each other to become an integrated design.

Both of the pieces shown in Figs. 6-17 and 6-18 are rectangular in form, but there the resemblance ends. Mr. Warsinski has produced a simple statement in a beautiful mohair cinch rope that has a soft sheen. On the other hand, Dolores Schiffert's hanging has been very skillfully divided into areas of pattern that have been knotted with several different knots. A detail of this hanging is shown in Fig. 2-55, page 24.

Although both works in Figs. 6-19 and 6-21 employ curvilinear design, Jessie Johanson's bells are bold and simple while Val Marks' hanging is delicate and complex. In the more delicate piece, forms that are usually knotted very geometrically have been relaxed so that they are more sympathetic with the curvilinear design.

6-14

6-15

6-16

6-18

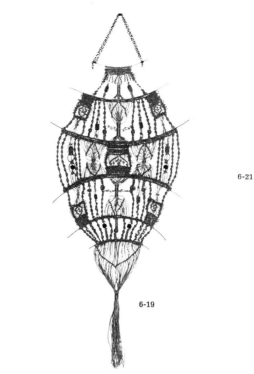

6-20

6-19

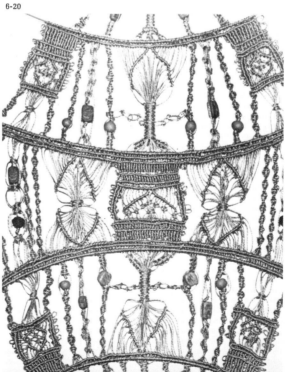

6-21

6-17. Norman Warsinski has used a welded metal form and mohair cinch rope for an elegantly simple hanging.

6-18. This monumental hanging that was knotted by Dolores Schiffert features Josephine Knots, Half Knot sinnets, and unknotted cords. (Photograph by Robert Lopez.)

6-19. Curvilinear design is featured in this hanging by Val Marks from Australia. (Photograph by Col Evans.)

6-20. Detail of 6-19. (Photograph by Col Evans.)

6-21. Jessie Johanson has used an interesting piece of curved driftwood and repeated the curve in pottery bells held by macramé sinnets.

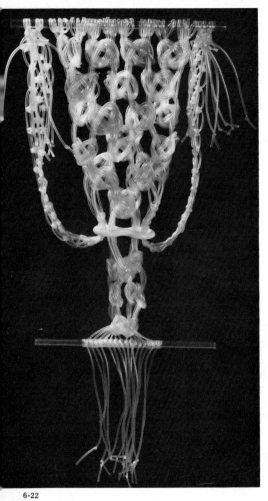

6-22

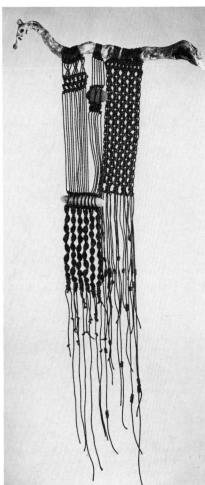

6-23

6-22. Plastic tubing and Plexiglas combine in an unusual hanging by Judith Hendry. (Photograph by Paul Macapia.)

6-23. Driftwood, a beach rock, and nylon seine twine form a simple composition by Jessie Johanson.

6-24. For the complete photograph of Mary Stephens Nelson's hanging, see Fig. 4-1, page 73.

6-25. J. I. Cochran knotted this handsome rug of heavy linen cord. Dimensions: 26″ x 38″. (Photograph by Kent Kammerer.)

6-26. Joan Michaels Paque's hanging, of which this is a detail, was knotted of polished cotton cord.

6-24

Man-made materials contrast with found objects. Judith Hendry has combined some unusual man-made materials into an interesting hanging that features Josephine Knots. (See Fig. 6-22.) Jessie Johanson's hanging (Fig. 6-23) makes you long to spend a day at the beach with some knotting cord in hand. Her design has sympathetically combined man-made seine twine with natural materials.

An open pattern of simple design makes for a handsome composition in Mary Stephens Nelson's hanging (see Fig. 6-24) whereas the knotting in Fig. 6-25 exhibits density of knots and a clean-cut geometric design. Contrast between fine and heavy knotting cord is dramatically illustrated by comparing the hanging with the varied patterns within the geometric space division in Fig. 6-26 with the delicate pattern of the pillbox hat in Fig. 6-27. The open pattern and more casual design of the transparency shown in Fig. 6-28 forms a striking contrast to the denser pattern of the charming bedspread rack in Fig. 6-29.

Both works shown in Figs. 6-30 and 6-32 have been knotted with beautiful precision, but otherwise they have little in common. Glen Kaufman (Fig. 6-34) and Carol Robinson (Fig. 6-35) have both used a circular form in their pieces, but the similarity ends there.

6-25

6-26

6-27

6-28

6-29

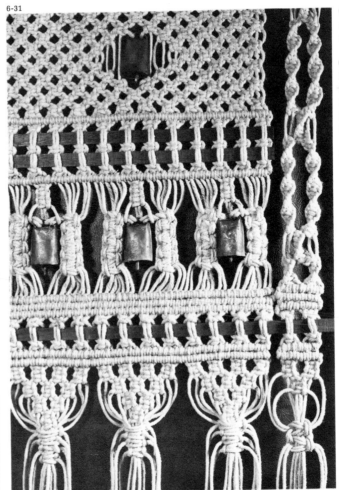

6-27. This pillbox hat was knotted of a soft green nylon stitching twine by Ellice Seelye.

6-28. A rose-blue wool hanging by Edith Henzer, who was a pupil in a textile course taught by Marlise Staehelin in AGS Basel, Switzerland. (Photograph by Hans Isenschmid.)

6-29. "The Titi Tree" by Win Tucker is a beadspread rack that might also be useful as a screen. (Photograph by Al Georgeson, Foley Studio.)

6-30. "Teak Strips with Spanish Sheep Bells" by Gerald P. Hodge was knotted with upholsterer's linen spring twine in natural color. Dimensions: 25" x 66". (Photograph by Michael V. Przekop.)

6-31. Detail of 6-28. (Photograph by Michael V. Przekop.)

6-32. "Horse" by Ron Franks is made of white clothesline with wood balls and an iron ring. Approximately 36" across. (Photograph by Darrell Meuthing.)

6-33. Detail of 6-32. (Photograph by Darrell Meuthing.)

6-32

6-33

6-34. "Lunar Totem" by Glen Kaufman was knotted with white cotton over Plexiglas. Dimensions: 24″ x 10″. (Photograph by Richard DiLiberto.)

6-35. In this hanging pot by Carol Robinson, Square Knot and Half Knot sinnets into which beads have been inserted are used to suspend the pot. (Photograph by Lincoln Potter.)

6-36. Detail of 6-35. (Photograph by Lincoln Potter.)

6-34

6-35

6-36

6-37

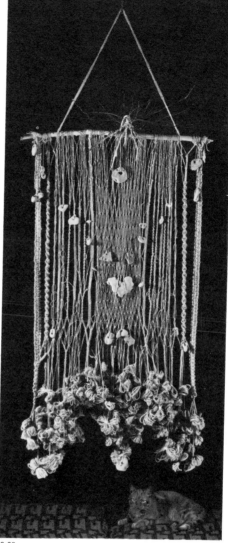

6-38

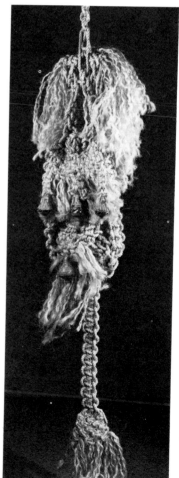

6-39

Although both Carol Robinson's and Else Regensteiner's hangings are symmetrical in design, the open, casual air of Mrs. Regensteiner's work (Fig. 6-38) differs greatly from the denser, more precise character of Carol Robinson's piece (Fig. 6-37).

By stretching the imagination, Lucy Driver's hanging (Fig. 6-39) could be a hairy neighbor of Gerald P. Hodge's sleepy-eyed creature (Fig. 6-40) in two more works that demonstrate great contrast in the styles of knotting.

The list of examples could go on, but hopefully the foregoing chapters and illustrations will suffice to spur the knotter on to experimentation, self-expression, and, above all, fun in macramé — in all of which design and color play such a vital role. This book was meant to whet the reader's appetite, and to aid him in undertaking new, exciting macramé projects; if it does this, it will have accomplished its purpose.

6-40. "Mask with Monkey Fist Fringe" by Gerald P. Hodge was made of black upholsterer's spring twine. Dimensions with fringe: 18″ x 71″. (Photograph by Michael V. Przekop.)

6-41. Detail of 6-40. (Photograph by Michael V. Przekop.)

6-40

6-41

BIBLIOGRAPHY

DESIGN

Bevlin, Marjorie Elliot. *Design Through Discovery* (2nd ed.). New York: Holt, Rinehart and Winston, Inc., 1970.

Moseley, Spencer; Johnson, Pauline; and Koenig, Hazel. *Crafts Design, An Illustrated Guide.* Belmont, California: Wadsworth Publishing Company, Inc., 1962.

Proctor, Richard. *The Principles of Pattern for Craftsmen and Designers.* New York: Van Nostrand Reinhold Company, 1969.

Scott, Robert Gillam. *Design Fundamentals.* New York: McGraw-Hill Book Company, Inc., 1951

COLOR

Birren, Faber (editor). *A Grammar of Color, a Basic Treatise on the Color System of Albert H. Munsell.* New York: Van Nostrand Reinhold Company, 1969.

————. *Principles of Color, a Review of Past Traditions and Modern Theories of Color Harmony.* New York: Van Nostrand Reinhold Company, 1969.

———— (editor). *The Color Primer, a Basic Treatise on the Color System of Wilhelm Ostwald.* New York: Van Nostrand Reinhold Company, 1969.

Hickethier, Alfred. *Color Mixing by Numbers.* New York: Van Nostrand Reinhold Company, 1963.

Itten, Johannes. *The Art of Color.* New York: Reinhold Publishing Company, 1961.

INDEX

Page numbers in italics indicate illustrations.